Ulysses Green Escapes

HIKING IN QUÉBEC

Yves Séguin

Ulysses Travel Publications

Series Director Claude Morneau	*Correction* Tracy Kendrick	*Illustrations* Jean-François Bienvenue
Project Director Pascale Couture	*Contributors* Mathieu Arcand Daniel Desjardins	*Photography* Daniel Rousse
Author Yves Séguin (Physical Educator)	Gérald Pomerleau Carol J. Wood	*Cartography* Jean-François Bienvenue Suzanne Châles
	Graphic Design Jean-F. Bienvenue	André Duchesne
English Translation Jennifer McMorran	Pierre Daveluy	

Special Thanks to: Guy Avon, Andrée Badeau, Nicole Blondeau, Lise Boudule, Jocelyne Campeau, Chantal Chrétien, Pierre-Denis Cloutier, Lucille Dazé, Sylvain Geneau, Marie-Josée Guy, Francine Joncas, Elyse Lauzon, Mona Longpré, Daniel Martin, Paul Perreault, Luc Poirier, Normand Sharkey.

Distributors

CANADA :
Ulysses Books & Maps
4176 Saint-Denis
Montréal, Québec
H2W 2M5
☎ (514) 843-9882
Fax : 514-843-9448

GREAT BRITAIN :
Roger Lascelles
47 York Road
Brentford
OH 45202
☎ 847-0935
Fax : 568-3886

U.S.A. :
Seven Hills Book Distributors
49 Central Avenue
Cincinnati, Ohio, 45202
☎ 1-800-545-2005
Fax : (513) 381-0753

GERMANY :
Brettschneider Fernreisebedarf
GmbH
D-8011 Poing bei München
Hauptstr. 5
☎ 08121-71436
Fax : 08121-71419

NETHERLANDS and FLANDERS :
Nilsson & Lamm
Pampuslaan 212-214
Postbus 195
1380 AD Weesp (NL)
☎ 02940-65044
Fax : 02940-15054

SCANDINAVIA :
Scanvik Books Imports
Esplanaden 8B
DK-1263 Copenhagen K
DENMARK
☎ 33 12 77 66
Fax : 33 91 28 82

Other countries, contact Ulysses Books & Maps (Montréal), Fax : (514) 843-9448

Canadian Cataloguing in Publication Data

Séguin, Yves, 1961-

    Hiking in Québec
    (Ulysses Green Escapes)
    Translation of : Randonnée pédestre au Québec
    Includes index.

ISBN 2-921444-42-9

1. Hiking - Quebec (Province) - Guidebooks. I. Title. II. Series.

GV199.44,C22Q813   1994   796.5'1'09714   C94-941259-7

*"Today I have grown taller
from walking with the trees."*

Karle Wilson Baker

TABLE OF CONTENTS

LIST OF MAPS

Help make Ulysses Travel Guides even better!

The information contained in this guide was correct at press time. However, mistakes can slip in, omissions are always possible, places can disappear, etc. We value your comments, corrections and suggestions, as they allow us to keep each guide up to date.

The best contributions will be rewarded with a free book from Ulysses Travel Publications. All you have to do is write us at the following address and indicate which title you would be interested in receiving (see the list at the end).

Ulysses Travel Publications
4176 - rue Saint-Denis
Montréal, Québec
Canada H2W 2M5

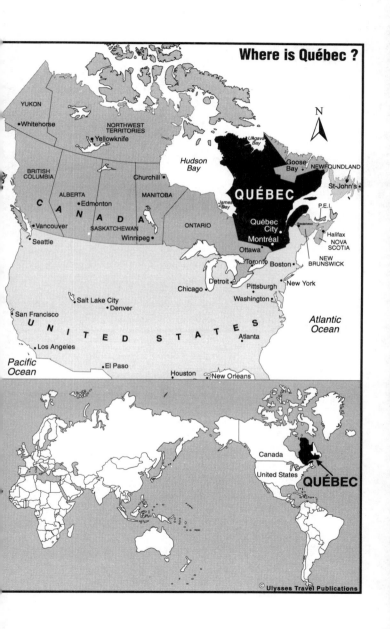

Where is Québec ?

YUKON
• Whitehorse

NORTHWEST
TERRITORIES
• Yellowknife

BRITISH
COLUMBIA

• Vancouver

• Seattle

C A N A D A

ALBERTA
• Edmonton

SASKATCHEWAN

MANITOBA

Churchill •

Winnipeg •

Hudson
Bay

Ungava
Bay

James
Bay

QUÉBEC

Goose
Bay

NEWFOUNDLAND

St-John's •

P.E.I.

Québec
City •

Montréal •

ONTARIO

Ottawa •

Toronto •

Boston •

Fredericton

Halifax •

NOVA
SCOTIA

NEW
BRUNSWICK

Chicago •

Detroit •

Pittsburgh •

New York •

• Salt Lake City
• Denver

Washington •

• San Francisco

U N I T E D   S T A T E S

Atlantic
Ocean

• Los Angeles

• El Paso

Houston •

Atlanta •

New Orleans

Pacific
Ocean

N

Canada

United States

QUÉBEC

© Ulysses Travel Publications

QUÉBEC AND HIKING

The aim of this hiking guide is to help hikers discover the most beautiful and picturesque trails in the Québec. As such not every walking and hiking area is included, only a carefully selected, well trodden few.

While providing important information for beginners (distances, times, costs, addresses, food, safety and rescue, etc.), this guide also informs the experienced hiker with an extensive choice of less known, but very interesting trails.

We have also sought to satisfy those who prefer walking to hiking, by presenting a good selection of shorter easier trails, especially near the large urban centres.

Following the publication of the Ulysses Green Escapes Guide *Hiking in the Northeastern United States* (in French and in English), several readers requested a similar guide for Québec. The author initially replied that there simply were not enough hiking trails in Québec to warrant such a guide.

However, while working as a researcher for the French-language television programme *Oxygène* (a programme dealing with outdoor activities and adventures in Québec, produced by Productions La Sterne) he discovered the immense potential of hiking in Québec. He realized that each of the regions in Québec was covered with several hiking opportunities just waiting to be discovered.

Happy trails to you....♪ ♪

Hiking is definitely not something new in Québec. The first trails lead generally to various rock-climbing walls in Québec, and members of the Canadian Mountain Club (CMC), founded in 1949, were already using these trails. Shortly thereafter trails were cleared, marked and maintained in the Laurentides, Charlevoix, Saguenay and Gaspé regions.

On October 15, 1974 the Comité Québécois des Sentiers de Randonnée (Québec Hiking Trails Committee) was created. This later became associated with the Fédération Québécoise de la Raquette (Québec Snowshoeing Federation) and became Sentiers-Québec (1978, Québec Trails). Then, in 1983 the group became known as the Fédération Québécoise de la Marche (Québec Hiking Federation).

■ The Fédération Québécoise de la Marche

The Fédération Québécoise de la Marche (FQM) works to rally together all walking enthusiasts (hiking, city-walkers, speed-walkers, etc.) in order to promote the activity in all its forms.

The FQM no longer qualifies for government funding, and therefore relies on memberships for its survival and development. The annual fee ($20 per person, $25 per family) includes a subscription to the french-language magazine *Marche*, published four times a year, discounts at certain outdoor and camping stores and on products sold by the FQM. FQM staff can also answer all your questions on hiking, or refer you to the right place.

The FQM is run solely by volunteers, no one is paid! This is just one indication of the kind of devotion these people have to the promotion of hiking in Québec. Therefore if your call is not returned the same day, be patient and give them the benefit of the doubt. And if you would like to volunteer one, two or twenty hours of your time per week, do not hesitate. It is for a good cause, and you will meet some interesting people.

Once a year the FQM organizes a walking jamboree. This is a great opportunity to explore a new corner of Québec, and to meet some of the folks who run the FQM.

The FQM's offices are located at 4545 Avenue Pierre-de-Coubertin, in Montréal, ☎ (514) 252-3157.

The National Trail

The National Trail project (called the Sentier National in Québec) was born in 1977, and intends to link Canadian hiking trails from the Atlantic to the Pacific! One day, the completion date is the year 2000, hikers will walk some ten thousand "uninterrupted" kilometres from Newfoundland to British Columbia!

The Québec portion of the National Trail (or Sentier National) is under the control of the Sentier National au Québec (SNQ) committee, founded in 1990. This committee of volunteers is affiliated with the Fédération Québécoise de la Marche.

The National Trail in Québec is expected to cross seven regions, Outaouais, Laurentides, Lanaudière, Cœur-du-Québec, the Québec City region, Charlevoix and Bas-Saint-Laurent. Of the 1,000 km of trails planned, more than 100 km have been inaugurated so far (with another portion scheduled for opening in October of 1994), in the Outaouais, Laurentides and Lanaudière regions.

The call once again goes out to volunteers to help with the project. To join the Sentier National Québec committee contact the Fédération Québécoise de la Marche at ☎ (514) 252-3157. Réal Martel is the project coordinator.

Hiking and Walking Clubs

People usually hike with family or in couples. There are however several hiking clubs in Québec. There are two main reasons people join hiking clubs, first of all to get motivated and force themselves to just get up and go, and secondly to meet people who share the same interest in physical activity.

It is best to shop around for the right club, since there are clubs for all tastes; walking in the city, walking indoors, speed-walking, endurance hiking, mountain hiking, excursions, clubs for singles, for the elderly, etc.

Get in contact with the Fédération Québécoise de la Marche at ☎ (514) 252-3157 to find a club in your area that offers what you want. Several CÉGEPS (junior colleges) and universities have their own outdoor clubs and often organize hiking trips.

The following is a list of some clubs that organize hiking trips: Accès Sentier, Détour Nature, Ecole de Plein Air Zahra, JASS, Parc Ami Chic-Chocs, Parc Sutton, Randonnées Plein Air, Randonneurs du Mont Yamaska, Randonneurs du Saguenay, Sentiers de l'Estrie, Y.M.C.A. Downtown, etc.

■ Starting a Hiking Club

Many people prefer to start their own hiking club. With the help of a few friends it is relatively easy to delegate the jobs: car-pooling, safety, telephone numbers and calling, etc. The bigger the club gets the more planning and confirming are necessary.

In order to simplify the job of starting your own hiking club, big or small, Nicole Blondeau of the Fédération Québécoise de la Marche has written a booklet (in French only) with all the steps to follow to found a successful club.

The Sentiers de l'Estrie

The Sentiers de l'Estrie (SE) club is a non-profit organization that manages and maintains a 130 km-long network of trails in the Estrie (Eastern Townships) region. This linear trail, the longest in Québec, goes from Kingsbury to the American border (south of Sutton), passing across magnificent Mont Orford, Mont Glen, Mont Echo and Mont Sutton along the way.

The club also organizes guided trips, maintenance hikes (to clean up the trails), snowshoe and cross-country skiing trips.

To inform yourself before hitting the Sentiers de l'Estrie (SE) trails, hikers should purchase the topo-guide published by the SE, available in travel bookstores and outdoor and camping stores. The guide describes the seven different zones of the Sentiers de l'Estrie trails and how to get to each one. Hikers find their way around thanks to the minute details (viewpoints, distances, access roads, campsites, parking etc.) that are well explained in the guide.

For more details write to Sentiers de l'Estrie Inc., C.P. 93, Sherbrooke, Québec, J1H 5H5, ☎ (819) 829-1992.

Centres Éducatifs Forestiers (CEF)

The Centres Éducatifs Forestiers (CEF, Forestry Education Centres) of Québec are not very well known, even in Québec. And what an unfortunate oversight, since these little gems have so much to offer!

If you have you ever wondered about the name of some plant or tree, the usefulness of a specific insect, how animals spend the winter, what is a microclimate or an ecosystem, etc., the CEF are there to answer all of these questions, or at least give you the tools to find them out yourself.

There are nine Centres Éducatifs Forestiers (CEF) spread out across the province of Québec. The centres were created during the seventies, thanks to the intervention of the Québec Ministry of Energy and Resources.

The first goal of the CEF is to increase people's knowledge and appreciation of the forest in the hopes of bringing them closer to nature. This is done discreetly, while respecting the hikers' need for knowledge. There is no need to join a group, since all the information is presented in such a way that visitors guide themselves.

Each CEF has a Pavillon d'Interprétation, or information centre, an exhibition hall, a documentation centre as well as a network of well laid-out trails oriented toward the natural phenomena of the forest and the area. Most of the trails are short and easy, very easy actually. This is an ideal spot to bring young children. Several CEF also offer trails that have been laid out to accommodate physically handicapped people.

Different activities are organized in the Pavillons d'Interprétation (information centres) and on the trails. Groups can also take advantage of the personalized services of a naturalist-guide. Entrance, parking and all services offered in the different CEF are free.

Unfortunately the CEF were all closed in April of 1994. They will eventually be reopened and managed by private groups. At press time only the CEF des Laurentides (see p?) had been reopened, so be sure to call ahead if you would like to visit another centre.

Quiz: Hiking in Québec

True or False...

1   The highest mountain chain in Québec is the Torngat.

2   The McGerrigle Mountains are located in Parc du Mont-Tremblant.

3   The Centres Éducatifs Forestiers (CEF, Forestry Education Centres) are reserved for children.

4   Hypothermia begins when the internal body temperature falls below 36 °C.

5   Clothing insulates the body from the surrounding air.

6   There are very few mosquitoes in the Estrie (Eastern Townships) region.

7   A "long" hike is over 10 km.

8   Bringing children under six years of age on a hike is not recommended.

9   Drinking water before a hike is a bad idea.

10   A cairn is a rustic lean-to.

11   The skin irritation appears immediately following contact with poison ivy.

12   It is better to wear several layers of clothing than just one.

13   On a topographic map, the closer together the contour lines are, the steeper the slope is.

14   Parc Forillon is a national park.

15   Parc d'Aiguebelle is located in the Montérégie region.

16   The population of great white geese in the Réserve Nationale de Faune du Cap Tourmente has reached more than 30,000.

17   Down filled sleeping bags dry faster than those insulated with synthetic materials.

18 The Sentiers de l'Estrie (SE) trails form a 130 km loop.

19 On a topographic map north is at the bottom of the map.

20 The Parc des Hautes-Gorges-de-la-Rivière-Malbaie has walls of rock over 700 m high.

21 There are more than 300 km of beach in the Îles-de-la-Madeleine.

22 While on safaris in Parc de Grands-Jardins, moose and wolves can be observed.

23 Walking downhill is often more strenuous on the muscles than walking uphill.

24 Île aux Lièvres is located in front of the city of Trois-Pistoles.

25 Cuts are the most frequent injury when hiking.

26 The Canadian National Trail will link the Pacific and Atlantic.

27 The Saguenay fjord is one of the 20 longest in the world.

28 Lipids should constitute the largest percentage of your daily intake.

29 The Groulx Mountains are located near the Baskatong Reservoir.

30 Excess vitamins are discarded by the body in the urine.

Answers at the end of the guide, p 165

HIKING

H iking is an aerobic activity; it is therefore normal for breathing to fluctuate at the beginning of a hike, as the amount of oxygen being consumed increases rapidly. When consumption of oxygen stabilizes so do breathing and heart rate.

The physical benefits of hiking are obvious. First of all, at the cardio-vascular level, the size and capacity of the heart increase. As a result, the volume of blood pumped through the body and the heart rate increase. Even though the resting heart rate decreases, the amount of oxygen supplied to the body actually increases because the heart is able to distribute blood to active muscles more efficiently.

Aerobic training reduces systolic and diastolic pressures (blood pressure) at rest and during light exercise, particularly among those with hypertension. Over time these developments allow us to do the same hike again and again, each time feeling better than the last.

The psychological benefits of hiking are less obvious, but no less significant. Everyone who hikes or walks regularly (hiking on weekends and walking during the week) will notice positive changes in their outlook. In the outdoors a simple existence brings us in touch with nature and back to the basics. Meditation, observation, and clean crisp air all lead to a clear state of mind. We return from a hike refreshed, rejuvenated, and relaxed.

French climber Yves Pollet-Villard once said of the mountains, "Up there we find ourselves." Life seems simpler and more harmonious, far from the madding crowds of urban life, leaving the mind clear for endless possibilities.

The Physiology of Walking

Simply put, hiking is walking. That, however, is where the simplicity ends. There are countless ways of walking and countless different types of terrain to walk on. The amount of energy spent during a walk varies significantly with the walking surface. Just as walking on pavement is not at all like walking on snow or sand, so walking on the sidewalk is not at all like trekking over the rough terrain you will find on a mountain hike.

Hiking in the mountains involves, aside from the occasional flat stretch, walking uphill and walking downhill.

■ Walking Uphill

Unlike walking on a flat surface, where the oscillation of the centre of gravity is what propels us forward, walking uphill requires a constant push against gravity. The foot has a tendency to place itself flat and directly below the centre of gravity. This position requires that the ankle be fully extended and often results in shin pain or injury. The upper body leans forward in an effort to balance the centre of gravity. The muscles of the knee and hips also have to work harder in order to carry the hiker uphill against gravity.

■ Walking Downhill

Going downhill requires a constant braking against gravity. This "negative" work puts an enormous strain on the muscles and tendons of the leg. The centre of gravity must be kept behind the forward leg, which requires leaning the body back, slowing down the descent.

The leg must be placed forward slowly until it touches the ground and then, by bending the knee, the centre of gravity is carefully shifted downwards.

Walking downhill, since it requires this constant braking with the lower body, is often much more strenuous on the muscles than walking uphill. Running downhill, especially when carrying a backpack, is not recommended and can even be dangerous.

■ Carrying a Load

Usually the hikers are not carrying only their own weight up and downhill. Depending on the length of the hike, most hikes require transporting some extra weight. Longer hikes can mean up to an extra 25 kg.

The weight of hiking shoes can also make quite a difference, since it takes much more energy to carry extra weight on the feet than on the upper body.

■ Rhythm

Experienced hikers know how to pace themselves. It is important to remember not to set out on a trail too fast, yet to maintain a pace that requires some exertion. Do not give up at the smallest sign of fatigue. Allow some time for your body to adjust to the physical demands being placed on it.

Experience will also help each hiker develop his or her own rhythm with respect to taking breaks. Most experts advise a ten minute resting period after each hour of walking. Try not to stop every fifteen minutes since at that rate the body does not have a chance to adjust to the exertion. During a hike, snacks and especially water are a must. You should be drinking almost continuously even if you're not thirsty, so practise your simultaneous walking and drinking.

■ Training

Arriving at the summit of a mountain is much more pleasant if you are not tired and out of breath. You will appreciate the break much more, eat with a hearty appetite, relax and look forward to the hike down. Physical fitness is essential to enjoying a good hike, and to eventually attempting some more difficult ones. It is not necessary to train intensively three hours a day, lift weights, or follow a strictly regimented diet. There are many little tricks that help to build up physical endurance.

The essential is of course walking. Walking three times a week for an hour each time, maintaining a relatively quick pace, (but not so fast as to make conversation impossible) is the best way to train. Within a couple of weeks you will easily quicken your pace and walk comfortably even with a loaded backpack.

Activities like biking, jogging, cycling and cross-country skiing are all aerobic activities and therefore also excellent ways to train for hiking.

Some simple changes to your daily routine will actually make a significant difference to your level of physical fitness. If possible try walking or riding a bike to work. Walk to the grocery store and, if the bags are too heavy use a backpack. Take the stairs instead of the elevator. Take a short walk after eating lunch. Watch television while riding a stationary bike. Every little bit helps.

■ Walking and Weight Loss

A lot of people exercise with the sole purpose of losing weight. If this goal also leads them to the mountains, then all the better, since the most difficult part is getting into some sort of routine, actually getting out and daring to go. From the first few successful outings you will discover the benefits and joys of hiking.

Walking and hiking are excellent physical activities that promote weight loss. They require intensity and endurance, both of which are essential to controlling body weight. The intensity, or rhythm should be moderate (not too slow) and the duration of the activity quite long. This combination forces the body to draw the energy it requires from fat deposits in the body.

People who like to snack in between meals will find the following experiment interesting. The next time you feel hungry go for a walk first. Once back from your walk not only will you feel more relaxed, you may even notice that you no longer feel hungry.

It has been found that hunger is often a result of higher stress levels. The difference between people with weight problems and those without is generally not an issue of how much food they eat, but rather how they spend their energy. Going on a strict diet is not sufficient to really bring your weight down; some sort of exercise is necessary.

If your diet is already well balanced, and you want to lose weight, cutting down your food intake is not a good idea. An increase in the intensity and regularity of exercise is more effective. The same principle holds for someone looking to maintain a specific weight.

■ Body Temperature

Normal body temperature is 37°C (96°F). While hiking, this temperature is maintained by putting on and taking off excess clothing, by drinking plenty of water, and by paying attention to your rhythm.

An experienced hiker will have no qualms about alerting their companions of any risks (heat stroke, hypothermia, etc.).

Eating

A review of the basics tells us that a balanced diet is essential. The quality of the foods you take in on a daily basis influences your level of physical fitness. When hiking, food should be your first consideration. Heading out without any food is a big mistake that will almost certainly ruin your day, and potentially place you in danger.

■ How Much Do You Need?

The amount of energy required by the body varies with age, sex, and the type of physical activity. Someone in their twenties burns about 2,200 calories during an average day. In the mountains, on a long hike, that same person will burn as many as 5,000 calories. It is therefore essential to eat more in order to compensate, but it is also essential to eat sensibly.

■ What Do You Need?

Carbohydrates

Carbohydrates effectively provide the energy necessary for exertion. There are two types of carbohydrates: simple carbohydrates and complex carbohydrates. The first kind are found in sweets (chocolate, pastries, jams, etc.). Since they are digested by the body very quickly (one hour), they should make up only 10% of your daily intake of carbohydrates. Complex carbohydrates are found in foods like bread, pasta, rice, and grains. They are digested more slowly (two to six hours) and therefore provide a more constant source of energy. It is important to eat complex carbohydrates. They should make up approximately 55% of your daily intake of food.

Lipids

Lipids are either animal or vegetable fats. Animal fats should only make up one third of the total intake of fat, and vegetable fats the other two thirds. In total only 30-35% of the daily intake of calories should be from lipids. Animal fat is found in meats, butter, whole milk, cheese, and prepared foods like cold cuts. Vegetable fat is found in oils, margarine, dried fruits and chocolate. Lipids contribute significantly to the energy available to your body by protecting vital organs, maintaining body temperature, and transporting vitamins.

Proteins

Proteins are the building blocks of the body. They are responsible for the construction and repair of tissues in the body. They provide energy in extreme cases, such as malnutrition or fasting. As with lipids there are animal and vegetable proteins. Animal protein is found in meats and dairy products, while vegetable protein is found in cereals and legumes.

Minerals and Vitamins

Eating a balanced diet should take care of your vitamin and mineral needs. Excess vitamins are not stored in the body, but eliminated in the urine.

Water

While hiking in the mountains our bodies dehydrate at a much faster rate, and usually without our being aware of it. It is a good idea to get into the habit of drinking water regularly, even if you are not thirsty. Drink plenty of water before, during and after a hike to help your body rehydrate as quickly as possible. Each hiker should have their own one-litre water bottle. Water makes up 60% to 70% of body mass and has many functions: it regulates body temperature, transports minerals and vitamins and eliminates waste.

Throughout North America, including several regions of Québec, water sources are contaminated by the parasite *Giardia Lamblia* which causes intestinal problems like diarrhea. Many call it "Beaver Fever" because the parasite is carried into the water by beavers.

To avoid these symptoms the water must be treated by boiling it for two to three minutes and by adding iodine tablets. One could also treat it by passing it through a filter designed for such purposes (this is effective but costly). For one-day hikes, carrying bottled water from home should suffice. Get in the habit of checking the water quality with the park staff, or the organization that manages the trails.

A Few Important Tips

- Food should be easy and quick to prepare (for ex. pre-cooked rice, instant oatmeal).
- Weight and volume should be minimized (get rid of as much packaging as possible, chop up vegetables ahead of time).
- Each meal should be individually wrapped.
- Starting a meal with hot soup is good idea since it will quickly replenish the salt and water lost during the day.
- The evening meal is important since your evening and next day depend on it.

■ Short Hikes

For a short hike of one day it is particularly important to ensure a high carbohydrate intake. Your body requires the energy immediately and carbohydrates provide it most effectively. Breakfast should be complete and well-balanced. Instead of stopping and eating a big lunch, snack along the way and during short breaks. "GORP" (good old raisins and peanuts) or trail-mix, a mixture of dried fruits and nuts is a high-energy snack that can be munched on as you hike. Drinking a lot of water will also maximize your energy.

Suggestions

- Tomato and lettuce sandwiches
- Chopped vegetables
- Fresh fruit
- Cheese
- Fruit or nut cake
- Trail mix, "GORP"
- Water or unsweetened juice

■ Long Hikes

On longer hikes a more balanced menu is necessary to avoid missing any essential nutrients. Priority should be given to carbohydrates since they provide about 60% of your daily calories and therefore 60% of your energy.

Suggestions

Breakfast:

- Oatmeal with brown sugar, powdered milk, and dried fruit
- Cream of wheat
- Muffins

- Pita bread, bagel, english muffin
- peanut butter, jams, etc.
- coffee, tea, hot chocolate

Lunch:

- Dried or sliced meats, vegi-pâté
- Cheddar cheese or cream cheese
- Heavy bread (bagel)
- Fresh and dried fruit
- Raw vegetables
- Fruit or nut cake
- Mixed nuts

Supper:

- Soup
- Vegetables and rice
- Couscous
- Pasta
- Cheese fondue
- Instant pudding
- Herbal tea or hot chocolate

Two books that wil help you plan outdoor meals are:

- *The Canada Food Guide*
- *The One-Pan Gourmet: Fresh Food on the Trail* by Cliff Jacobson, how to cook outdoors, plan meals, recipes, etc.

First Aid

■ Typical Outdoor Injuries

It is important to be self-sufficient in the outdoors. As well as taking care of food, clothing, and shelter, you should also be equipped to handle any unforeseen snags — such as an accident that requires immediate attention. A first aid kit is an indispensable tool to ensure that your hike is a safe one. It should be simple and contain only the material you are likely to need, appropriate to the kind of light injuries likely to occur during a hike, usually blisters and sprains.

Blisters are most often the result of new shoes or of shoes that are too big. Before the blister actually develops cover the area with a piece of moleskin (sold in pharmacies). If the blister has already formed, pierce it and drain out the liquid. This allows the blister to dry out and heal more quickly. It is important to disinfect the blister and surround it with moleskin to avoid any further rubbing and irritation.

A sprained ankle occurs when the internal or external lateral ligaments are stretched. There are three types of sprains:

- A minor sprain is the most frequent type. The foot is twisted severely but there is no cracking sound nor immediate swelling. If the ankle is wrapped in a supportive bandage, the foot can be walked on until the closest rest area is reached. The pain will nonetheless be quite sharp.

The ankle should be iced as soon as possible. A cast is not necessary. In fact, the sooner one starts to walk on the ankle, the sooner it will heal itself.

- In the case of a moderate sprain the ligament is stretched and partially ripped. The cracking sound and inflammation that follow within the half hour make it easy to spot. The injured person will experience serious pain and will not be able to walk at all.

Ice or snow should be applied immediately and the injured person should be supported until a rest area is reached. The victim should stay off the injured ankle for 48 hours. On the third day the ankle, supported by a tensor bandage, can be walked on again.

- In a severe sprain the ligament is completely torn. The pain is intense and swelling occurs instantaneously. The injured person will be completely incapacitated, and the foot will turn blue immediately.

Before moving the injured person, immobilize the ankle. Support the person completely until a rest area is reached. A cast will be necessary and the injury may take several weeks to heal.

■ Hypothermia

It is easy to discount the cold when hiking in the month of July. However in the mountains, rain and wind can lower the temperature considerably. Imagine sitting above the tree line in a downpour, with the wind blowing at 50 km/h. Then imagine that you are tired and have no raincoat. In such conditions your body temperature drops rapidly and you run the risk of hypothermia.

Hypothermia starts when your internal body temperature falls below 36°C, when the body loses heat faster than it can produce it. Shivering is the first sign that your body is not able to warm itself. This signal should warn you to put on more clothing and to eat in order to replenish body's caloric energy.

There are six stages of hypothermia.

Stage 1 (37°C to 35°C): beginning to shiver, stumbling or tripping without reason, reduced manual dexterity.

Stage 2 (35°C to 32°C): shivering is much more marked and speech is often interrupted by violent trembling; the pulse and breathing rate increase; the skin becomes pale.

Stage 3 (32°C to 30°C): blood pressure, pulse and breathing decrease; coordination of movement is difficult because of the increasing stiffness of the muscles, speech becomes confused and the victim will stumble.

Stage 4 (30°C to 27°C): confusion, incoherent thoughts, semi-consciousness, stiff muscles, and dilation of the pupils.

Stage 5 (27°C to 25°C): loss of consciousness, cardiac irregularities, and coma.

Stage 6 (less than 25°C): cardiac and respiratory failure, oedema and pulmonary hemorrhage. At this stage, the victim is not far from death.

Hypothermia is very serious. Even though the weather may not seem to present any risks, it is important to bring along enough food, water and warm clothing.

■ Poison Ivy

Poison ivy is found in most natural regions of Québec. Unfortunately this harmful plant is difficult to recognize because it can adopt many contradictory characteristics: climbing or not, shiny or mat leaves, and differently coloured leaves depending on the season. All parts of the plant contain the offending oil (toxicodendrol) which is transmitted when it comes in contact with skin or clothing. The rash appears 24 to 48 hours after contact. The symptoms include painful itching, reddened skin, and bumps which become blisters. A victim of poison ivy should consult a physician.

Three little tricks for identifying poison ivy:

- The leaves are in groups of threes.
- The stem of the centre leaf is longer than that of the other leaves.
- The middle vein of the leaf is off-centre.

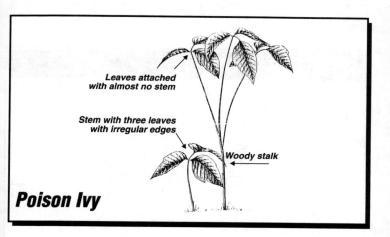

*Leaves attached
with almost no stem*

*Stem with three leaves
with irregular edges*

Woody stalk

Poison Ivy

■ General Safety Tips

- Leave early (better to return at 2 p.m. than 9 p.m.).
- Give your complete itinerary to someone (friend, parent, spouse, etc.).
- When in a group, always wait for others at intersections.
- When in a group, take a head count often.
- Keep pace with the slowest person in the group.
- Stay on the trails.
- Do not underestimate the difficulty of the hike, or overestimate your abilities.
- Plan the hike at home, in advance.
- Always keep track of where you are on a map.
- Bring extra clothing, food and water.
- Bring a strong loud whistle.
- Use a topographic trail map and bring a compass (and know how to use it!).

Orientation

When hiking you will usually be following marked trails. Generally, hiking does not involve off-trail orienteering or require a compass. For most, the task of orientation requires little more than an understanding of the information provided by topographic trail maps. It is rare that you will have to use a compass on marked trails, except perhaps to identify a summit in the distance or to orient yourself in bad weather.

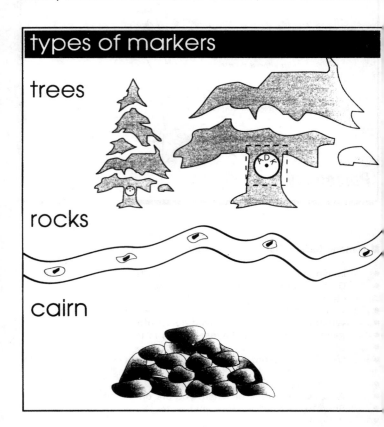

types of markers

trees

rocks

cairn

■ Marked Trails

Marked trails are usually identified by cairns, small signs or paint markings on trees or rocks. A cairn is a type of marker frequently used on bare mountain tops. It is essentially a pile of small boulders, about one metre high, indicating the trail to follow.

Markers are spots of coloured paint on rocks or on the ground. The colour remains consistent for the duration of a given trail. The markers are spaced evenly so that it is easy to tell if you are on the right track. In case of doubt it is best to return to the last marker and pay special attention to the surroundings to make sure you are heading in the right direction.

■ Topographic Maps

Topographic maps (from the greek *topos*, place and *graphien*, to draw) are representations of a specific area of land drawn from aerial photographs. They show the relief of the land, as well as the distance and change in altitude between two points.

This information is crucial when hiking because the level of difficulty of a hike depends on the steepness, or slope, of the terrain much more than on the total distance covered.

A well-prepared hiker will have topographical maps which include existing trails. In Québec, most maps are distributed by the parks or the organizations that maintain and manage the trails. Several of these maps are available from the Fédération Québécoise de la Marche (☎ 514-252-3157) or from the government through the Ministère de l'Evironnement et de la Faune.

Bring along a clear plastic case for maps to protect them from humidity and rain, (zip-lock freezer bags work well) or better yet buy them plasticized. Some maps are available made of a water-resistant, tearproof material.

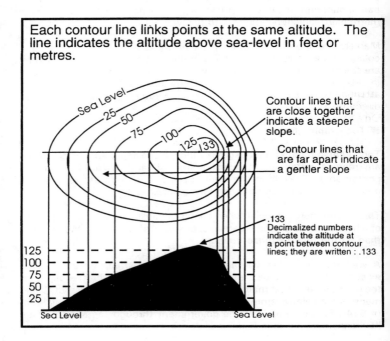

Each contour line links points at the same altitude. The line indicates the altitude above sea-level in feet or metres.

Sea Level

25

50

75

100

125 / 133

Contour lines that are close together indicate a steeper slope.

Contour lines that are far apart indicate a gentler slope

.133
Decimalized numbers indicate the altitude at a point between contour lines; they are written : .133

125
100
75
50
25
Sea Level   Sea Level

Topographical maps provide much more information than regular maps, and it is worth the effort to read through it all, especially the legend, usually located in the margin. The colours of the symbols follow certain topographical conventions:

> black = man-made objects
> blue = water (streams, rivers, lakes)
> green = vegetation
> brown = relief (irregularities of the terrain)

The contour lines are the lines on the map, usually drawn in brown, which indicate the mountains, hills and valleys. The space between each line represents a specific and constant change in altitude (in feet or metres), such that the farther apart the contour lines, the less steep the terrain, and vice versa (see illustration).

The cardinal points should be indicated on a topographical map. Unless otherwise stated north is at the top. There should also be a scale so that distances can be measured. When trying to measure a trail from the map it is easier and more accurate to use a piece of string than a ruler. Use the string to measure the curved trail line and then measure the length of string used.

■ Distance and Time

On a flat surface humans walk between 3.2 and 6.4 km/h. Going uphill this changes to between 1.6 and 3.2 km/h. There is an easy way to calculate the length of a particular hike: assume one hour for every 3 km covered and add an extra 1/2 hour for each 300 m of change in altitude. Take for example, a hike of 6 km with a change in altitude of 900 metres: 1 x 6/3 km = two hours, 1/2 x 900/300 m = one and a half hours, for a total of three and a half hours. This formula does not take into consideration all the variables that could affect your walking speed, such as:

- general physical fitness;
- how often you walk, your ability to pace yourself;
- the load you are carrying (backpack, footwear);
- the weather (rain, snow, heat, humidity);
- the quality of the trail (steepness, clear to follow);
- your familiarity with the particular trail (have you done it before);
- the varying ability of each hiker (beginners, children, older people);
- the size of the group (frequent stops to rest, for water, for pictures).

■ Optional Trails

Once you have chosen to hike a specific trail, it is a good idea to check the map for other trails in the area that might serve as shortcuts or alternate routes in case of an accident to one of the hikers or bad weather conditions. These other trails might provide quicker access down the mountain in order to return to the departure spot and should be marked on your map with a grease pencil.

Climate and Temperature

The climate in the mountains is different from the climate at sea level. Up in the mountains weather changes are more frequent and less predictable. It is possible for a clear blue sky to darken all of a sudden and erupt into a fierce storm. Similarly, bad weather can disappear as quickly as it appeared.

There is generally more cloud cover at higher altitudes and a greater chance of precipitation. The explanation for this phenomenon is that warm air from the valley is able to absorb more humidity than the cold air at the top of the mountain. Air is forced up by the mountain. The air cools and can no longer support the humidity — the results are cloud cover, heavy fog and precipitation in the form of snow or rain.

Once the air has passed the summit it descends again into the valley, warms up and is able to spread out once again. The sky clears up and it is a beautiful day in the valley.

The higher the altitude the lower the temperature, usually about 1 °C per 180 m. The wind-chill factor can also lower the temperature drastically. In June or July, very cold temperatures have been recorded on Québec's highest summits, most notably in the Gaspé.

The top of a mountain is that much closer to the sun. Solar radiation (the brightness of the sun) rises approximately 3% per 100 m increase in altitude. A good pair of sunglasses, an effective sun-screen lotion, and a hat are essential. A blanket of snow will intensify the reflection of ultraviolet rays. Also remember that in the mountains the air is much thinner and drier.

■ Wind

In the mountains and on bare summits, wind is a significant factor. If there is a small breeze at the base of the mountain, you can be sure it is very windy at the summit. Not only does the wind make us work harder, it also has a dramatic effect on temperature. For example, if the temperature is 5 °C and the wind speed is 50 km/h, the real temperature (the temperature we feel) will be -12 °C. For this reason it is crucial to bring a warm sweater, an anorak, a tuque and gloves when you plan on heading uphill, even if it seems like a great day.

Wind Velocity KM/H	Temperature in Celsius (°C)									
	10°	5°	-1°	-7°	-12°	-18°	-23°	-29°	-34°	-40°
0km/h	Temperature with windchill factor(°C)									
	10°	5°	-1°	-7°	-12°	-18°	-23°	-29°	-34°	-40°
8	9	3	-3	-9	-14	-20.5	-26	-32	-37.5	-44
16	5	-2	-9	-15	-23	-29.5	-36	-43	-50	-56.5
24	2	-6	-13	-20.5	-27.5	-37.5	-43	-50	-57.5	-64.5
32	0	-7.5	-15	-23	-32	-39	-47.5	-55	-63	-70.5
40	-1	-9	-18	-26	-34	-42	-51	-58.5	-66	-75
48	-2	-11	-19	-27.5	-36	-44.5	-52.5	-61	-69.5	-78
56	-3	-11.5	-20	-29	-37	-45	-55	-63	-72	-80
64	-3.5	-12	-21	-29.5	-38	-47.5	-56	-64.5	-73	-81.5
	Normal winter conditions. Little danger provided appropriately dressed for weather.				Increased danger		Very dangerous			
					Freezing of exposed body parts.					

 ## Accommodations

Québec has a wide selection of accommodations to offer hikers. We have listed seven of these, one or all of which are available in the regions covered.

Self-Serve and Free

- tent camping
- tarpaulin
- bivouac under the stars

Organized

- shelter
- lodge
- lean-to
- private campground

A complete list of most campsites (government run and private) is available free of charge from the organization called Camping Québec (☎ 1-800-363-0457) or from the various Québec tourist associations (☎ 1-800-363-7777).

To make reservations in Québec's provincial parks call ☎ 1-800-665-6527.

■ Tent Camping

Many areas, particularly in parks, have designated areas where camping is permitted. It is usually possible, depending on the place, to camp next to shelters.

■ Tarpaulin

Camping under a tarpaulin shelter involves suspending the tarp between four trees. This allows the excitement of sleeping outside, while at the same time providing some protection from the elements. Tarpaulins are available in different sizes, can accommodate quite a few people and are inexpensive. A rainy, windy night presents some problems since the rain is easily blown through the sides of the shelter. A tarpaulin also protects the campfire or campstove from rain, or it could serve as an eating area in the case of a long stretch of rainy days.

■ Bivouac Under the Stars

Sleeping under the stars is another possibility. It may sometimes be necessary to bivouac, or tuck yourself into a cramped, uncomfortable spot in the event of bad weather. Some hikers bring along small bivouacs for sleeping bags (water-proof bags that fit over the sleeping bag).

If you plan to sleep outdoors it is essential to bring some sort of ground sheet (that may double as a poncho) to keep your sleeping bag dry.

A bivouac is ideal for those intrepid hikers who want a taste of the real outdoors. However sleeping in the open air presents a few inconveniences and some precautions should be taken. Be sure to stay relatively close to a shelter, in case you need to return in the middle of the night. You should also avoid changing the site of your bivouac once it has been determined.

■ Shelters

Shelter, called *refuges* in Québec, are basically rustic cabins in which you are expected to be self-sufficient. In other words, you must provide your own food and warmth. These are available for hikers particularly in Parc de la Gaspésie, Parc du Mont-Tremblant and along the Inter-Centre trails.

■ Lodges

These are more comfortable than shelters, and are common in Québec where they are called *gîtes*. Sleeping in a lighthouse on one of the islands of the Bas-Saint-Laurent, with meals included, would fit into this category.

■ Lean-Tos

A lean-to, called an *abri* in Québec, is a structure with three walls and a sloped roof. Even though one side is completely exposed, it still provides protection from wind and rain. Popular in the United States, these are less common in Québec.

■ Private Camping

Camping in privately-run campgrounds close to the trails is another possibility. You should look for loop trails since each night you will be returning to the same site. Private camping is often referred to as deluxe camping. It is ideal for families, older people or anyone who wants to be assured of a comfortable sleep. Keeping your baggage to a minimum becomes less important since your car is always nearby.

■ Choosing a Campsite

There are two reasons to avoid picking a mountain summit as a campground. First, the fragile mountain vegetation can be damaged by too much foot traffic. Second, temperatures are much lower on bare mountain summits which have no wooded areas to shield you from high winds.

When contemplating a particular site ask yourself, "Do I have permission to camp here?". You should find the answer before arriving at a site by contacting a visitor centre (of the park, municipality, organization, etc.) or by referring to a topographical map on which campsites are usually indicated.

Night will invariably have begun to fall by the time the site has been chosen, with the tent, fire, water, etc. still to be taken care of. The best way to get things done quickly and efficiently is to divide the tasks.

It is important to set up camp, and dig your toilet, at least 50 m from the nearest water source to avoid contamination. Never wash dishes directly in the water source, even if you are using biodegradable soap, but rather in a container. Again be sure to dump the waste water at least 50 m away from any water source.

The same rule applies when your are cleaning yourself. Never do so in the water source, even with biodegradable soap. Use a washcloth instead.

Hiking Etiquette Tips

Each hiker is one among millions. If the forest appears untouched, it is in part thanks to those who have passed before. As a hiker you should always make sure that the nature and beauty that you enjoy on a hike are preserved out of respect for hikers who will follow, and of course out of respect for nature itself. The environment is something that must be respected and protected.

This respect means sticking to the trail, since foot traffic can severely damage fragile mountain vegetation, even if there is snow on the ground. Also, do not hike on mountain bike trails.

Build fires only in designated areas and only with dead wood. Never cut firewood from living trees (live wood does not burn well anyway!). Whenever possible, prepare meals on a campstove, rather than a campfire. If a fire is absolutely necessary, make sure it is thoroughly extinguished when you are finished.

Equally important is to camp only in designated areas, bring all your garbage with you when you leave (aluminum and plastic do not completely burn), do not throw anything into the water source (soap, urine, food, etc.), and do not feed the animals. Not only is this safer for you, it also shows respect for the animals.

Hikers should also be respectful of the group. Accept the pace of the slowest member, and the fatigue of others, so that everyone remains in good spirits. It is important to pull your own weight, pitch in as much as possible, and respect the needs of others for peace and quiet.

Often in a large group the most experienced member may be unofficially appointed the leader. This does not mean this person has the last word or may not welcome other ideas. Try to keep it democratic.

■ Domesticated Animals

Domesticated animals are not permitted in most parks in the Québec, and bringing your pet on the trails with you is strongly discouraged. Nevertheless, it is a good idea to check with the park regarding the specific rules and regulations for the area you will be visiting.

Organizing a Hike

A short one-day hike does not pose too many difficulties. It is important, however, not to overlook the aspect of security. In other words,
bring along a first aid kit, warm clothing, a flashlight, etc., just in case.

For longer hikes of two or more days with a group of people, preparing
ahead of time is a must. At least one week in advance, organize a
meeting with the entire group. This meeting will serve to get everyone
well acquainted, to plan everything, to distribute the jobs, and, finally,
to get everyone enthusiastic.

The following specifics should be worked out at this meeting:

- introduction of each member (name, experience, expectations);
- choice of itinerary (with topographical maps);
- menu decision (high energy, quick and easy to prepare);
- organization of equipment for the group (tent, campstove, etc.);
- each member's personal gear;
- proper clothing for each member;
- selection of a group leader (especially if most of the group is inexperienced);
- trouble shooting for potential problems (weather, distances, etc.);
- reservations, if necessary;
- review of everyone's knowledge of orienteering, first aid, survival techniques, etc.;
- division of tasks (shopping for food and equipment);
- organization of transportation;
- review of everyone's state of health (those with allergies, heart conditions, diabetes, etc. should make the group aware of their conditions before the hike);
- exchange phone numbers.

Hiking and Children

There is no ideal age for hiking. Even children less than three years old
can gain something... as long as there are willing arms to carry the
little adventurer. Child-carrying backpacks are widely available in hiking
and camping stores.

Beyond the age of three or four, children should have no problem
walking the distance... but only if they want to! The concept of
distance is inconsequential to a child; the prospects of discovery and
adventure are what motivate them! However as soon as a hike ceases
to be fun, the little hiker will most probably also cease to move. It does

not take much to break the spell, so it is a good idea not to venture too far from the car, or to be sure a strong back and shoulders are always available.

Older children and young adolescents like to pick and choose. At this age parents should include the children in some of the preparation and of course some of the responsibilities. Even better would be to sign up for an orienteering class with your child to develop their and your interest in hiking.

Adolescents may be hard pressed to leave the gang for a weekend in the great outdoors with Mom and Dad, so why not bring the whole gang along (within reason of course)! A longer hike complete with an overnight in tents or a shelter is a great way to show young adults how "cool" the outdoors and hiking really are!

Here are a few tips for a successful hike with children.

- Choose short and easy hikes with a high interest factor (such as self-guided or interpretational hikes).
- Hike before noon, leaving the afternoon open for the beach, etc.
- Protect children well from sun (sunhat, sunscreen), rain and mosquitoes.
- Make sure they drink water or juice constantly.
- Think of some games or songs for the hike (hide and seek, games with the compass, etc.).
- Leave extra space in the backpack for souvenirs.
- Follow the children's pace.
- Take short breaks.
- Prepare high-energy, tasty snacks.
- Encourage children to take photographs.
- Allow them to explore and climb (safely).
- Show interest in their discoveries (frogs, toads, worms, beetles, etc).
- Remember to bring along a younger child's favourite stuffed animal or toy.

Equivalents

	Metric	Imperial
Length		
	1 cm	0.3937 in.
	1 m	3.281 ft.
	1 km	0.6214 mi.
Weight		
	1 g	0.035 oz.
	1 kg	2.205 lb.
Area		
	1 m^2	10.76 ft^2
	1 km^2	0.386 mi^2
	1 ha	2.47 acres
Volume		
	1 L	0.22 gal.
	1 L	0.26 gal. us

Imperial	Metric
1 in.	2.54 cm
1 ft.	0.3048 m
1 mi.	1.609 km
1 oz.	28.35 g
1 lb.	453.69 g
1 ft^2	0.093 m^2
1 mi^2	2.59 km^2
1 acre	0.4049 ha
1 gal.	4.545 L
1 gal. us	3.785 L

■ Temperature

To convert :
°F to °C : subtract 32, divide by 9 and multiply by 5.
°C to °F : multiply by 9, divide by five and add 32.

EQUIPMENT

S hopping for equipment can be half the fun of preparing for a hike, and as with many other things you may find yourself tempted to follow fashion trends. In recent years equipment has become modernized. The clothing is more chic, the boots are lighter and the accessories are more sophisticated. This trend has certainly made hiking more visually attractive. More importantly it has made hiking more comfortable. Of course, innovation automatically costs more, and hiking is no exception.

For many this financial obstacle will be no obstacle at all, but for others such an investment is hard to justify. Most hikers start with basic equipment, and find it is no hindrance to their enjoyment of hiking. As long as you are comfortable and safe you can easily hike the same trail as the hiker who is decked out in top-of-the-line gear.

Hiking is not for everyone, so before you spend a fortune on costly equipment take a few test runs. There are places in the major centres of Québec where you can rent equipment (see Equipment Rental p 49).

This will help you decide what gear you need and save you money in the long run.

The small snags encountered on your first hikes will determine what equipment is best suited to your needs, and help you distinguish between what is essential, what is superfluous, and what is useful but can wait.

The Essentials

Here are some descriptions of what is available:

■ The Backpack

Up until a couple of years ago there were two types of backpacks on the market: external frame packs and internal frame packs. The former have virtually disappeared from the market, mainly as a result of improvements in the construction of internal frame packs, which are much lighter and easier to adjust to the body.

A good backpack should have the following:

- A well-padded waist belt;
- compression straps along the side of the bag to decrease the volume of the bag and to keep the weight of the bag close to the body;
- the possibility of adjusting the length of the bag between the belt and the shoulder straps to fit the back;
- compartments on the outside of the bag;
- about 60 to 70 L of volume (the larger bag, the greater the temptation to fill it);
- eyes and straps to which items may be attached;
- a clasp across the chest to join the shoulder strasps together.

When packing, always start with the sleeping bag at the bottom. Next add things you will not need through the course of the day, such as the campstove and clothing for the evening and night. Finally, on top, put the clothing and essentials you will need as you hike. It is important to put the heaviest gear, which is usually the food, two thirds of the way down into the bag. The mattress can be attached between the bag and the pocket on top, strapped to the side, or if the backpack is big enough, placed inside. In this case roll the mattress up and place the equipment in the middle of it.

Attaching things to the outside of your backpack is generally not a good idea, as they disrupt your balance and can get caught on branches.

For one day hikes a small backpack (about 30 L) is sufficient. It should be big enough to carry a water bottle, camera, first-aid kit, maps, compass, food for the day and extra clothing. Check that it is solid, especially the shoulder straps.

■ The Sleeping Bag

As it does for clothing, the insulating ability of the sleeping bag depends on the thickness of the insulation. The thicker the bag, the warmer it will be. At the same time, however, bags of varying weights may offer the same insulation value. For example a down-filled bag is lighter than a bag insulated with "Polarguard". However, down-filled bags lose their insulation value when wet and take a long time to dry. Also in Québec's humid climate down presents a problem, unless the shell of the bag is made of a breathable fabric (like "Gore-Tex"). It is therefore a better idea to buy a bag insulated with synthetic materials that dry faster and are more reliable in wet weather, even though it may be heavier and cost more.

Mummy bags are warmer because they eliminate the extra space between your body and the bag, space which eventually fills with cold air. There are different sizes of sleeping bags so do not hesitate to try them on in the store. A bag with a temperature rating of -5°C is sufficient for summer (-12°C for spring and fall).

It is important to check that the zipper is protected by a flap which prevents cold air from blowing into the bag. If the sleeping bag takes up too much room in the backpack, use straps to compress it and decrease its volume.

Proper care of your sleeping bag will ensure that the insulation lasts. To avoid deterioration of the insulation do not store the sleeping bag rolled up or stuffed into its sack. Take it out after each trip and keep it on a hanger.

These are the synthetic insulations available today: "Polarguard", "Hollofil" and "Quallofil". For the same weight "Quallofil" provides the most warmth.

■ The Insulating Mattress

These mattresses are essential if you want to take full advantage of the insulating capability of your sleeping bag. On a long hike it is impossible to carry a large, heavy, inflatable air mattress. Small, clo-sed-cell air mattresses are therefore ideal. They are lightweight, waterproof, and easily attached to the exterior of the pack. They are available in three thicknesses, 0.75 cm, 1 cm, and 1.5 cm. Also available are small inflatable air mattresses that insulate well and are very comfortable, but expensive.

■ The Tent

To be effective a tent must keep out wind, rain, and bugs. It also has to be quick and easy to set up, and big enough to offer basic comfort. If it has no pegs you can move it around after it is assembled. Arched frame pegs joined by elastic make it easier to mount the tent. In order to maximize space you may want to add a vestibule where bags and gear can be kept. Finally, the tent should be light and compact: about 3 kg for 2 people, and approximately 3.5 kg for 3 people. A good tent will have a double roof, or fly, of waterproof nylon with waterproof seams. The fly should rest far enough above the tent so as not to touch it. It should also come far enough down the sides of the tent to properly protect it from wind. The screen of the tent must be fireproof and large enough to provide sufficient ventilation.

■ The Campstove

The most important considerations here are efficiency and weight. Efficiency means the amount of time it takes to boil a litre of water. Stoves that use naphthalene are generally more efficient, but they require more maintenance and are often difficult to light in cold weather.

Alcohol burning stoves are more practical. They are easy to light, work in any temperature, and require little maintenance. Their main drawback is the difficulty of adjusting the flame. Butane stoves are also practical, but, like the naphtha-fuelled type, are inefficient in cold weather.

■ The Mess Kit

Many portable stoves come complete with a mess kit. If this is not the case you will need to buy pots, but make sure they don't take up half your bag. Usually a kit comes with a multi-purpose handle for moving hot pots, and a set of dishes and cups. The dishes and cups should be plastic so that food does not cool too quickly. Large plastic mugs are available that insulate and have tops. They are inexpensive and keep things warm longer. A pocketknife, fork, spoon and a handkerchief will complete your travelling kitchen.

■ The Water Bottle

A one litre water bottle with a large neck is ideal. It is easier to fill without getting your hands wet, and the opening will not freeze as quickly in cold weather (look for the "Nalgene" brand). Avoid using leather gourds. They give a foul taste to the water and will eventually soak through to your backpack. To avoid frozen water, place the bottle in your backpack so that it is against your back. Your body heat will keep the water liquid.

■ The Compass

A compass is not essential when you are following marked trails. You may want to bring one along in case of emergency or just for fun. Since hiking is not orienteering, you do not need a hi-tech model. A simple "Sylva" compass ($10 to $15) will do the job. A compass will allow you to orient your map properly in the absence of any visible landmarks. Once at the summit it will also allow you to identify other mountains in the distance.

It is a good idea to have some information on how to use a compass or to follow a course (check with outdoor club or school, or with the Fédération Québécoise de la Marche at ☎ 514-252-3157). Otherwise ask an experienced friend to give you some pointers before heading out.

■ The Flashlight

The ideal flashlight is one that can be worn on the head like a miner's lamp or headlamp. It leaves both hands free to do other things like eating, putting up the tent, going to the bathroom, etc.

■ The Repair Kit

The repair kit must be versatile. With few materials you should be able to repair big items, at least temporarily. The kit should contain supplies for the stove, some copper wire, a small sewing kit, a small pair of pliers, and a pair of shoelaces.

■ Footwear

Depending on the type of hiking there are three types of footwear.

Walking shoes are useful for light hiking trips of one day on groomed trails without steep inclines. They generally do not do well in humid conditions, and so are not ideal for the adventurous hiker.

Half shoe, half boot models will allow you to conquer some more imposing peaks on one-day hikes by providing more ankle support than walking shoes do. They are adequate for hikes of more than one day, but your ankles will begin to feel it, especially on a rough trail toting a backpack weighing a few kilos.

Light hiking boots are useful for all hikes. They are higher and stronger than the other two types and therefore sufficient for mountain hiking and for hiking on rough, uneven trails. These boots do not however provide protection from cold or snow.

When trying on boots in the store remember the following advice.

- Bring the socks you will be wearing when you hike (polypropylene or cotton, and wool socks).
- Make sure there is no excess pressure on the top of the foot.
- Walk around with the shoes on for at least 10 minutes in order to get a genuine idea of how they fit.
- "Gore-Tex" boots are waterproof to a point. Do not believe that they will *always* keep you dry.
- A pair of gaiters over the boots will keep your feet dryer for longer and will also keep out little pebbles.
- Treat leather and other boots with "Sno-seal", or another beeswax protector before wearing them.

Clothing

As much as you need to cover yourself up at night you should also pay close attention to your day clothes, in order to maintain the ideal body temperature (37°C). What you wear in all types of weather and at all times of the day is crucial. Clothing insulates and protects the body from the surrounding air; it protects you from the heat and from the cold.

Water is a good heat conductor. It is therefore important to wear clothes that breathe, meaning that they keep you warm while at the same time allowing perspiration to evaporate. In the case of anoraks (Gore-Tex or otherwise), you want something that lets the sweat out and also keeps the rain from coming in.

Fleece or "Synchilla" are very useful in this respect. They insulate well and dry more quickly than wool. Layering is the best way to dress when hiking. You can take off or add layers as your body warms and cools, without too drastic a change.

Never wait until you start sweating before removing a layer. Rather, take it off as soon as you begin to feel warm. A ski jacket is not a good idea because you will be too warm with it on and too cold without it.

Layers for the upper body should consist of the following:

- Undershirt that breathes (polypropylene, etc.);
- Fleece or wool sweater;
- Anorak (if it is not made of "Gore-Tex" or of similar fabric, it is better to have an anorak that breathes and a raincoat);
- Tuque;
- Mittens or gloves.

Layers for the lower body consist of:

- Long underwear that breathe (polypropylene, etc.);
- Lightweight, loose-fitting pants;
- Waterproof or "Gore-Tex" pants;
- Two pairs of socks, to avoid friction (one pair of polypropylene or cotton socks next to your skin and another wool pair);
- Gaiters.

Gaiters keep mud, rocks, snow and water from getting into boots. They also help to keep feet warm and to protect socks and pants from soiling. On long hikes, in rainy, muddy weather gaiters ($20 to $40) are indispensable.

■ Day Clothing

Day clothing is worn while actually hiking. Within this category there are cold weather and warm weather clothes.

Cold Weather

According to McArdle and Katch in *Exercise Physiology*, the weave of clothing fibres trap warm air against the body and therefore insulate from the cold. Since clothing and air are poor conductors of heat, they form a barrier against heat loss. The more air that is trapped against the skin, the better insulated it will be. This is why several layers of thinner clothing, or clothes lined with fur or synthetic fibres (made up of several layers of trapped air), provide better insulation than just one heavy winter jacket.

As soon as you begin to get chilled the first thing to add is a tuque or some sort of hat, since your body loses 30% to 40% of its heat through the head.

Dry clothes should be your priority in cold weather, since clothing dampened by rain or sweat loses 90% of its insulating capability. If you do not have an anorak to protect you from the rain ("Gore-Tex", "Dermoflex", etc.), you should bring a raincoat as well as a cotton or nylon anorak. Never forget to bring a tuque and gloves or mittens since evenings and mornings can be quite chilly at higher altitudes.

During the hike you will probably wear an anorak over your undershirt, whether warm or cool, keeping the fleece or wool sweater for rest stops, meals, and evenings.

It is not a good idea to wear jeans. Generally they are too tight, too heavy and take too long to dry. Cotton pants (or jogging pants), cotton/nylon pants, or corduroy pants, are better ideas. The warmest fabrics (in decreasing order) are wool, cotton, flannel and nylon.

Warm Weather

Most hikers find the heat more difficult to bear than the cold. This explains why there are fewer hikers on the trails of southwestern Québec during the month of July than in the fall.

Dressing for warm weather is not as easy as it would seem. Wearing shorts may be the most comfortable option, until you wander into low-lying brush and your legs get scratched. Ultra-light nylon pants are better.

Warm weather clothing must be ample to allow air to circulate between the fabric and your skin and to allow perspiration to evaporate. Colour is also important. Dark colours absorb more light and therefore more heat than light colours. Even with loose light-coloured clothing, your body will only cool down when your clothes become wet and the cooling evaporation can occur. According to W.D. McArdle, a physiology professor at the University of New York putting, on a new dry shirt in hot weather goes against the phenomenon of thermoregulation. He proposes that the loss of heat due to evaporation, which creates a cooling sensation, will only happen when your clothing is completely wet. Therefore to beat the heat it is better to keep your wet shirt on than to change it for a dry one, which would only put off the eventual cooling evaporation of your body's sweat.

■ Night Clothing

Dressing for nighttime is essentially the same as dressing for cold weather. It is especially important to dress warmly at night (even in the summer) because the body has a tendency to cool down after a long day of exercising. Also in the mountains the drop in temperature after sundown is much more significant. During the spring and fall most hikers find they need a down vest and slippers to sleep in.

Keeping warm at night is a priority. Without a good night sleep you risk wasting the morning in bed, or spending the day overtired.

What you actually wear while sleeping will depend on your sleeping bag. If you have a good bag, that is a warm one, you could sleep naked. If your bag's insulating ability is not high then it is best to get dressed for bed a while before actually going to bed. Leave your long underwear on (top and bottom) to maintain your body's warmth. A fleece or wool sweater may be needed in really cold weather, and of course remember to wear a tuque since most of your body heat escapes through your head.

Equipment Rental

Instead of purchasing all of the equipment necessary for long hikes, which can be quite costly, try renting out a few items (from camping stores, outing clubs, universities or CÉGEPS). Campstoves, mess-kits, backpacks, sleeping bags, saws, etc, can all be rented at reasonable prices, giving you the opportunity to decide what best suits your needs when it comes time to buy. You will also determine if you are the type of hiker who prefers to carry their life on their back for a few days, or perhaps the comforts of a well-stocked lodge are more your style!

■ Repairs

If your camping or hiking equipment needs breaks, before replacing it consider repairing it. In Montréal De Fil en Montagne, 3774 Rue Saint-Denis, ☎ (514) 848-1145, does good repair work.

■ Camping and Outdoor Stores Near Québec Hiking Trails

- La Cordée, 2159 Rue Sainte-Cathrine Est, Montréal, ☎ (514) 524-1106
- L'Aventurier Trailhead, 1604 Rue Saint-Denis, Montréal ☎ (514) 849-4100
- Mountain Equipment Co-op, 5 Beechwood Avenue, Ottawa ☎ (613) 745-1094
- Boutique La Randonnée, 292 Rue King Ouest, Sherbrooke, ☎ (819) 566-8882
- L'Aventurier, 710 Rue Bouvier, Québec, ☎ (418) 624-9088
- Azimut, 1194 Rue Cartier, Québec, ☎ (418) 648-9500
- Vélo Plein-Air, 324 Cathédrale, Rimouski, ☎ (418) 723-0001

■ One-Day Hikes

Clothing

- windbreaker
- wool sweater
- raincoat
- wind-resistant pants
- nylon pants
- small gloves
- gaiters
- polypropylene underwear
- t-shirt
- tuque

Equipment

- sunglasses
- toilet paper
- camera
- small flashlight
- knife
- water bottle

First-Aid Kit

- "elastoplast" bandages
- antibiotic ointment
- elastic bandage

■ Long Hikes

Clothing

- windbreaker
- wool sweater
- two t-shirts
- two sets of polypropylene underwear
- nylon pants
- wind-resistant pants
- 4 pairs of socks (cotton and wool or polypropylene)
- small gloves
- gaiters
- tuque
- hiking boots

Camping Equipment

- tent
- sleeping bag
- ground sheet
- back-pack

Kitchen Equipment

- campstove
- fuel
- mess kit
- pocketknife, forks, spoons
- small plastic plates
- plastic cups
- dish rag
- ecological steel wool

First-Aid Kit

- one pair of scissors
- sterile bandages
- butterfly bandages
- antibiotic ointment
- UV lip protector
- glucose tablets
- sterile tape
- moleskin
- pin, needle, blade
- sanitary napkins
- matches
- alcohol swabs
- aspirin

CLASSIFICATION OF HIKES

T he hikes suggested are organized according to level of difficulty: easy, difficult or very difficult. The levels are represented in the guide by the following symbol: ⌂

⌂	(easy):	short hike with little change in altitude.
⌂⌂	(difficult):	long hike with little change in altitude **OR** short hike with significant change in altitude.
⌂⌂⌂	(very difficult):	long hike with significant change in altitude **OR** extremely long hike **OR** hike with very large change in altitude.

Maps

The maps in this guide will help you to locate the specific area for each hike. However, **they are not topographical maps** and serve only to situate you with reference to towns and roads.

Long and Short Hikes

The terms long and short hikes, as they are used in this guide, do not refer to the total distance covered.

A short hike is one where the hiker returns to the starting point to sleep and so carries only a day pack containing lunch, water, sweater, anorak, camera, etc.

A long hike involves an overnight somewhere along the trail. The hiker must therefore carry all the essentials for two or more days, (food, clothing, campstove, mess-kit, sleeping-bag, tent, etc.).

Short hikes can still be quite demanding. Imagine, for example, leaving early one morning en route to Parc des Hautes-Gorges-de-la-Rivière-Malbaie, hiking to the summits of Acropole des Draveurs and Érables, returning to the car and driving home that evening. This little outing would require an early rise and a late night! On the other hand a long hike could be much less demanding if the distance covered and change in altitude per day were smaller.

The tourist regions of Québec

1. Îles-de-la-Madeleine
2. Gaspésie
3. Bas-Saint-Laurent
4. Québec City Region
5. Charlevoix
6. Chaudière-Appalaches
7. Cœur-du-Québec
8. Estrie (Eastern Townships)
9. Montérégie
10. Lanaudière
11. Laurentides

12. Montréal
13. Outaouais (Ottawa Valley)
14. Abitibi-Témiscamingue
15. Saguenay-Lac-Saint-Jean
16. Manicouagan
17. Duplessis
18. Nouveau-Québec-Baie-James
19. Laval

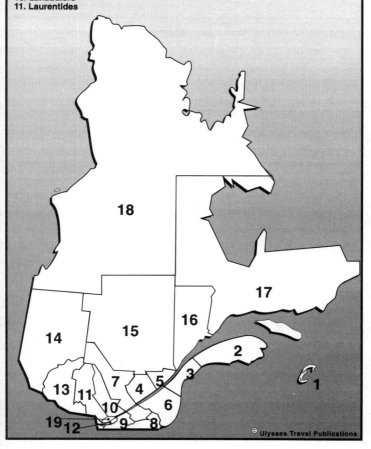

© Ulysses Travel Publications

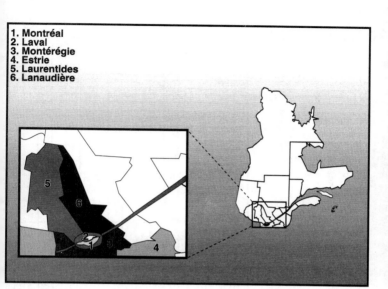

1. Montréal
2. Laval
3. Montérégie
4. Estrie
5. Laurentides
6. Lanaudière

MONTRÉAL AND REGION

Montréal's richly diverse urban landscape reflects the different stages of the city's evolution. There are three and a half centuries of tumultuous urban growth to explore, from the first colonial buildings in Vieux Montréal to the latest towers of glass and steel downtown. The splendour of the city's countless churches, the neoclassical façades of the banks along Rue Saint-Jacques, the small flat-roofed houses in the working-class neighbourhoods as well as the sumptuous mansions of the Golden Square Mile, are only some of the examples of Montréal's recent and not so recent history.

The unique and diversified regions in and around the city attract Montrealers with a virtually endless choice of green spaces to escape to, and plenty of opportunities to admire and appreciate the natural beauty that surrounds them.

MONTRÉAL AND REGION

	Level of Difficulty of Hike	Total Distance of Hike (km)	Change in Altitude (m)	Page
SHORT HIKES				
Parc de la Rivière des Mille Îles: Parcours du Héron	◺	3.0	0	63
Parc des Îles-de-Boucherville: Tour des Îles	◺	15.0	0	66
Parc du Mont-Saint-Bruno: Circuit n° 1 (Tour du Parc)	◺	9.0	100	67
Mont Saint-Hilaire: Pain de Sucre	◺	5.0	264	68
Mont Saint-Hilaire: Rocky	◺	8.7	255	68
Mont Saint-Hilaire: Dieppe	◺	7.0	229	68
Mont Saint-Hilaire: Burned Hill	◺	2.6	153	69
Parc Sutton: Roundtop	◺◺	4.6	420	72
Parc du Mont-Orford: Mont Chauve (Sentiers de l'Estrie)	◺◺	9.0	300	73
Parc du Mont-Orford: Mont Orford (Sentiers de l'Estrie)	◺◺	11.6	553	73
Mont Glen: Mont Glen (Sentiers de l'Estrie)	◺◺	8.4	275	74
Pic Chapman: Pic Chapman (Sentiers de l'Estrie)	◺◺	5.6	237	75
Parc de la Gorge de Coaticook: Tour du Parc	◺	3.0	50	76
Parc d'Oka: Sentier Historique du Calvaire d'Oka	◺	5.5	100	77
Parc d'Oka: Rivière-aux-Serpents	◺	1.8	0	78
Parc d'Oka: Sentier Écologique de la Grande-Baie	◺	3.0	35	78
Parc du Mont-Tremblant: La Roche et La Corniche	◺	8.0	250	80
Parc du Mont-Tremblant: Lac des Femmes	◺	2.7	60	81
Parc du Mont-Tremblant: Lac aux Atocas	◺	1.5	30	81

MONTREAL AND REGION	Level of difficulty of the hike	Total distance (km)	Change in altitude (m)	Page
Parc du Mont-Tremblant: L'Envol	◁	3.6	215	82
Mont Éléphant: Mont Éléphant	◁	7.0	240	84
L'Interval: Mont Legault	◁◁	6.0	330	85
L'Interval: Tour du Lac	◁	3.3	60	85
L'Interval: L'Érablière	◁	4.4	80	86
Chertsey: Le Sommet	◁	7.0	300	88
Chertsey: Mt-107	◁◁	7.4	380	88
Chertsey: Grande Vallée	◁◁	13.5	250	89
Matawinie: Sentier Matawinie (Sentier National)	◁◁	12.0	200	90
Matawinie: Côte à Monette	◁	5.0	100	91
Inter-Centre: Inter-Centre (Montagne Noire)	◁◁	14.0	450	92
Inter-Centre: Inter-Centre (Montagne Grise)	◁◁	17.0	400	92
LONG HIKES				
Parc du Mont-Tremblant: Pimbina	◁◁	28.2	425	82
Parc du Mont-Tremblant: La Diable	◁◁	45	250	83
Inter-Centre: Inter-Centre	◁◁◁	30	450	93

In keeping with the theme of a "Montréal recreational zone" we have chosen to include the tourist regions of Montréal, Laval, Montérégie, Eastern Townships (Estrie), Laurentides and Lanaudière in this chapter.

Montréal

In 1535, on his second expedition to North America, Jacques Cartier sailed up the Fleuve St-Laurent to the island of Montréal. He explored the shores and climbed Mont Royal. Cartier may not have been the first European to visit Montréal, but he was nevertheless the first to report its existence. Located at the confluence of what are today known as the Outaouais and St-Laurent rivers, the island was previously known by the Amerindians as Hochelaga. When Cartier visited the island for the first time there was a large fortified town at the foot of Mont Royal, with a population of around 1,000 Iroquoian Amerindians.

There are many beautiful hiking spots in and around Montréal, all accessible by bus or Métro, and all providing an escape to a natural setting that makes it easy to forget about the hustle and bustle of the city. The sights and sounds of nature are often only minutes from your doorstep; it is simply a question of discovering all they have to offer.

■ Parc du Mont Royal

Parc du Mont Royal was designed in 1874 by the American architect and landscape artist Frederick Law Olmsted, who is also responsible for the layout of New York City's Central Park. He was known for his ability to make the city more natural while at the same time urbanizing nature.

As well as many trails, Parc du Mont Royal offers a 1.5 km self-guided walk through the park. Spread out along the path are 15 stations which discuss three different topics: history, geology and flora and fauna. There is also an explanation of the use and function of the communication tower, the cross, the antenna, the chalet, etc.

From the observatory near the chalet, the magnificent view of the city, the Fleuve St-Laurent and the Montérégie hills spread out at your feet. You can even hike as far as the Cimetière Notre-Dame-des-Neiges. A list of the famous people buried in the cemetery is available. Keep an eye out for the tombstones of such notables as Émile Nelligan, Louis Fréchette, Alfred Laliberté, Louis-Hippolyte Lafontaine, Camilien Houde, Honoré Mercier, etc.

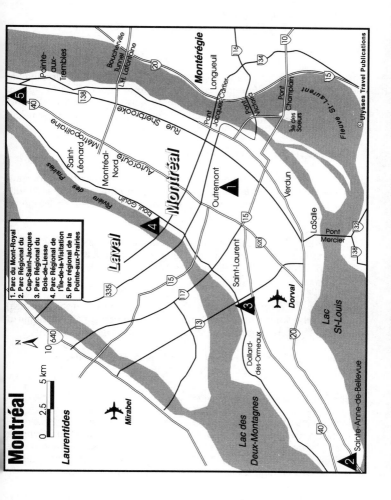

Montréal

Laurentides

N

0 2,5 5 km

1. Parc du Mont-Royal
2. Parc Régional du Cap-Saint-Jacques
3. Parc Régional du Bois-de-Liesse
4. Parc Régional de l'Île-de-la-Visitation
5. Parc régional de la Pointe-aux-Prairies

Mirabel

640 10

335

13

117

15

Lac des Deux-Montagnes

Dollard-des-Ormeaux

Sainte-Anne-de-Bellevue

40

Laval

Rivière des Prairies

boul. Gouin

Saint-Léonard

Montréal-Nord

Autoroute Métropolitaine

Rue Sherbrooke

Montréal

Outremont

Saint-Laurent

Dorval

20

520

Lac St-Louis

Verdun

LaSalle

Pont Mercier

138

32

Île des Soeurs

Pont Champlain

Fleuve St-Laurent

Pont Victoria

Pont Jacques-Cartier

15

Longueuil

Montérégie

34

116

10

15

20

138

40

5

Pointe-aux-Trembles

Boucherville Tunnel L.H. Lafontaine

© Ulysses Travel Publications

The cemetery also includes many magnificent specimens of trees rarely found in Québec.

    Centre de la Montagne ☎ (514) 844-4928
    Cimetière Notre-Dame-des-Neiges ☎ (514) 735-1361

■ Regional Parks

The Montréal Urban Community or MUC (Communauté Urbaine de Montréal, CUM, in French) is home to four regional parks *(parcs régionals)*, all of which are located on the north shore of the island of Montréal. These parks are veritable oases of greenery where you can walk and explore to your heart's content.

Parc Régional Cap-Saint-Jacques

This park is located in the northwestern part of the island of Montréal and has plenty to offer hikers and outdoor enthusiasts of all kinds. Water is everpresent in the park, which is shaped like an immense peninsula.

There are 27 kilometres of maintained hiking trails, as well as a self-guided nature trail. A magnificent fine sand beach (free admission) located on the Baie de la Pointe Madeleine, awaits hikers after their excursions.

The Centre d'Interprétation de la Nature (nature interpretation centre) located in the Château Gohier houses an exhibition on the ecology of the area. There is also an ecological farm with free admission.

Access: 20099 Boulevard Gouin Ouest, Pierrefonds.
              ☎ (514) 280-6871

Parc Régional Bois-de-Liesse

Bois-de-Liesse park is located on Boulevard Gouin, near Highway 13. The park is divided into two sectors (the Bois-Francs and the Péninsule sectors), thus offering abundant and richly diversified flora and fauna. The area is particularly suitable for bird-watching (with 130 species) and animal watching as well (beaver, fox, marmot, etc.).

Twelve kilometres of trails, studded with numerous stunning view-points, make it easy to explore the park. Each weekend nature-education activities (slide shows, guided tours, etc.) are organized by the park staff.

Access: 9432 Boulevard Gouin Ouest, Pierrefonds.
              ☎ (514) 280-6729, 280-6678

Parc Régional l'Île-de-la-Visitation

L'Île-de-la-Visitation park, located on Boulevard Gouin, near the
Papineau-Leblanc bridge, offers some beautiful hikes, which are mainly
of a historical nature. There is a lovely island, Île de la Visitation,
within the park, which is easy to cross and whose abundant vegetation
will quickly make you forget that you are still within the Montréal
Urban Community.

The 7 km of hiking trails throughout the park provide access to the
cross (on the island), the Maison du Meunier (the Miller's House) as
well as the Ancien Moulin (old mill), the Maison du Pressoir (the Press
House) and finally the superb Église de la Visitation. Constructed in
1750, it is the oldest church still standing in Montréal. More than 150
species of birds may be found in the park, and the Club d'Ornithologie
d'Ahuntsic, a birdwatching club, organizes regular outings.

Access: 2425 Boulevard Gouin Est.
              ☎ (514) 280-6733

Parc Régional Pointe-aux-Prairies

Pointe-aux-Prairies park is divided into four sectors, with trails leading
through everything from marshes to mature forests. The Pavillon des
Marais has an exhibit on the interpretation of the wetlands, and the
observation tower commands an impressive view of the whole region.
Guided hikes of the marsh area are also offered.

A section of the trails, 3.5 km long, is reserved exclusively for hiking,
while the other 12 km of trail are shared by bikers and walkers alike.

Access: 12300 Boulevard Gouin Est, or
              14905 Rue Sherbrooke Est.
              ☎ (514) 280-6691, 280-6688

Laval

The second largest city in Québec, Laval is located on a large island to
the north of Montréal, called Île Jésus. The island is washed by the
waters of Lac des Deux-Montagnes, la Rivière des Prairies and the Rivière des Mille Îles.

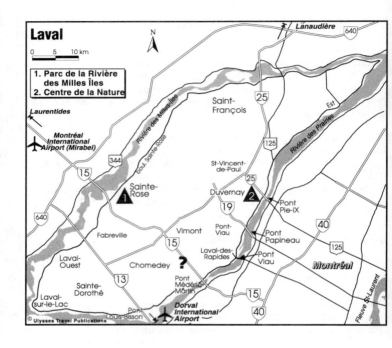

■ **Parc de la Rivière des Mille Îles**

Parc de la Rivière des Mille Îles came into existence in 1987 thanks to the efforts of the members of the *Corporation Éco-Nature de Laval*. The purpose of this group is to increase public awareness of the value of the environment and outdoor activities. The islands in the park can be explored by canoe and kayak (rentals available on site), as well as by foot, though you will need a canoe to reach them first.

Close to 5 km of self-guided nature trails enable hikers to familiarize themselves with the flora and fauna typically found in swamps and marshes. The park also provides guided tours dealing with the natural heritage and the history of the insular environment.

Access: Highway 15, Exit 16. Boulevard Sainte-Rose Est, just before Boulevard Curé-Labelle. Parc de la Rivière des Mille Îles, 345 Boulevard Sainte-Rose, Laval.
☎ (514) 664-4242

Parcours du Héron

Level of Difficulty:
Total Distance: *3 km*
Change in Altitude: *nil*
Starting Point: *Centre d'Interprétation (information centre).*

The Parcours de la Tortue (Turtle Trail) and the Parcours du Héron (Heron Trail) lead to Île des Juifs (Jew Island) by canoe or kayak; a 2 km hiking trail goes around the island. The next stop by water is Île aux Fraises (Strawberry Island), right nearby, for another walking tour (1 km). There are ten numbered lookout points along the Parcours du Héron, enabling visitors to familiarize themselves further with this string of islands.

■ **Centre de la Nature**

The Centre de la Nature de Laval is located right next to the Pie-IX bridge. This recreational park was created about 20 years ago on the site of an old quarry. Trees, green fields, gardens, a lake and a stream have transformed this ravaged land, into a beautiful area.

There are no specific hiking trails, but this is an ideal spot to bring young children for a walk or picnic. The distances are short, and the park is full of attractions; two gardens, a farm, a navigable lake, playing fields, picnic areas, activities, etc.

Access: 901 Avenue du Parc, Laval.
☎ (514) 662-4942

Montérégie

The six hills of the Montérégie region, Mont Saint-Bruno, Mont Saint-Hilaire, Mont Yamaska, Mont Rigaud, Mont Saint-Grégoire and Mont Rougemont, are the only significant land formations in this flat region. Scattered about irregularly here and there, these massive hills, rising no more than 500 m were long thought to be ancient volcanoes. In reality, they are masses of metamorphic rock that could not penetrate the earth's superficial crust, and were eventually exposed as the surrounding rock eroded.

The highlights of a visit to the Montérégie region are without a doubt the rolling hills, the lush Richelieu Valley with its rich historical heritage, and of course the fresh country air. The arrival of fall colours also signals apple-picking time in the Rougemont orchards.

■ Parc Régional de Longueuil

Parc Régional de Longueuil, on the south shore facing the island of of Montréal, offers numerous activities for amateur enthusiasts of ecology and the outdoors. Small lakes, rolling hills and walks through the forest await visitors. Over a hundred species of birds have been identified to date, and during the winter the deer sometimes come out for walks too.

Fifteen kilometres of hiking trails provide an opportunity to explore all the park has to offer.

Access: 1895 Rue Adoncour, Longueuil.
              ☎ (514) 646-8269

■ Parc des Îles-de-Boucherville

Parc des Îles-de-Boucherville was created in 1984. Located in the middle of the Fleuve St-Laurent, a few minutes from downtown Montréal, this park provides a haven of peace and quiet for urban nature-lovers.

The park consists of five islands linked together, which may be explored by foot or by bike. An educational brochure provides insight into the past and present of these islands.

So far more than 170 species of birds and 40 species of fish have been counted in the park. There are great views in every direction from the islands: from one side the port of Montréal with the backdrop of the Olympic Stadium and the skyscrapers of downtown, and from the other side the picturesque old section of the city of Boucherville.

Access: from Montréal, take the Louis-Hippolyte-Lafontaine
              bridge-tunnel, Exit 89.
              ☎ (514) 873-2843

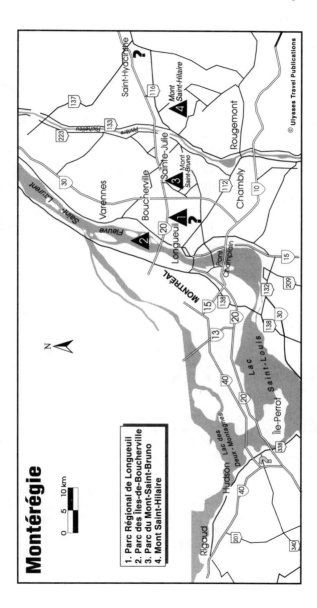

Montérégie

0 5 10 km

1. Parc Régional de Longueuil
2. Parc des Îles-de-Boucherville
3. Parc du Mont-Saint-Bruno
4. Mont Saint-Hilaire

© Ulysses Travel Publications

Tour des Îles

Level of Difficulty:	
Total Distance:	*15 km loop*
Change in Altitude:	*nil*
Starting Point:	*Poste d'Accueil (visitor centre) on Île Sainte-Marguerite.*

From the visitor centre, head toward the cable ferry that leads across to Île Pinard. From there Île de la Commune can be reached via a small bridge. The trail follows the St-Laurent, about 30 m from the bike path, then crosses over to Île Grosbois. It loops all the way around the island, then leads back to Île de la Commune and the cable ferry. At the beginning of the century, Île Grosbois housed an amusement park and a racetrack.

It is not necessary to go all the way around the island. There are several smaller loops, covering only a few kilometres, and the park staff will gladly recommend an excursion.

■ **Parc du Mont-Saint-Bruno**

This small park, which covers only 6 km², was created in 1985. The history of this land, however, goes back all the way to the 18th century, when it was known as the Seigneurie de Montarville.

Inside the park, there are no less than six beautiful little lakes, each flowing from one to the other. Mont Saint-Bruno stands just over 200 m. Near the visitor centre (poste d'acceuil), a lookout point offers a lovely view of downtown Montréal.

Thirty kilometres of trails trace their way through the park, and many short hikes are possible. The nature interpretation program is very diversified and includes apple cultivation, geological history, wildlife, human presence, maple groves, as well as the network of lakes and streams.

Access:	Parc du Mont Saint-Bruno is only 20 km from Montréal. Highway 20, Exit 102, then Chemin des 25 all the way to the park (330 Chemin des 25 Est, Saint-Bruno-de-Montarville).
	☎ (514) 653-7544

Circuit n° 1 (Tour du Parc)

Level of Difficulty:	⟨☖⟩
Total Distance:	*9 km loop*
Change in Altitude:	*100 m*
Starting Point:	*parking lot of the Poste d'Accueil (visitor centre).*

This trail loops around the entire park; simply follow the sign for "Circuit n° 1." A small detour off the trail is recommended to admire the Vieux Moulin (Old Mill, 1761) situated between Lac Seigneurial and Lac du Moulin. Farther along, the trail passes several small lakes then runs alongside an immense rock (the *Pierre de Lune* or lunar rock), a remnant of the glacial age. It then leads back to the visitors' centre.

■ **Mont Saint-Hilaire**

Mont Saint-Hilaire is a nature conservation centre. Located only 35 km from Montréal, it offers some beautiful hiking opportunities. The 24 km of trails are well maintained. Information about the flora and fauna, as well as the various trails, is available at the visitor centre.

In 1960 the federal government declared Mont Saint-Hilaire a refuge for migratory birds. In 1978 UNESCO declared it a "biosphere reserve", the first of its kind in Canada.

For many years the land was owned by a Mr. Hamilton Gault, who willed part of the mountain to McGill University in 1958.

Mont Saint-Hilaire has one of the most varied mineral compositions (more than 120 different types) in the world.

Solitary hikers need not feel lonely on Mont Saint-Hilaire: surrounded by about 600 species of plants, 178 species of birds, 41 species of mammals (but no bears), 12 species of amphibians and 13 species of fish, there is always more to learn!

Access:	Autoroute 20, Exit 113. Follow the signs for *Centre de la Nature*. Centre de Conservation de la Nature Mont Saint-Hilaire, 422 Rue des Moulins. ☎ (514) 467-1755

Pain de Sucre

Level of Difficulty:	⌂
Total Distance:	*5 km return*
Change in Altitude:	*264 m*
Starting Point:	*Pavillon des Visiteurs (visitor centre).*

The uphill section of this hike counts for only 2.5 km of the total, but it is quite steep near the end. The small exertion is rewarded at the summit of this *pain de sucre*, or sugarloaf, with a superb 360° view. Visible in the distance are the Rivière Richelieu, Mont Saint-Bruno, Mont Royal, and on a clear day the Laurentides mountains. Return by the same trail.

Rocky

Level of Difficulty:	⌂
Total Distance:	*8.7 km loop*
Change in Altitude:	*255 m*
Starting Point:	*Pavillon des Visiteurs (visitor centre).*

This trail passes close to Lac Hertel, climbs slowly up the north face, and then becomes quite steep on its way to the summit of Rocky (396 m). From there the trail descends a bit before heading up to the Sunrise summit (407 m). Finally, the trail zigzags back down to Lac Hertel and then back to the visitor centre.

Dieppe

Level of Difficulty:	⌂
Total Distance:	*7 km return*
Change in Altitude:	*229 m*
Starting Point:	*Pavillon des Visiteurs (visitor centre).*

This trail is a bit longer than the Pain de Sucre, but not as steep, and the terrain is more regular. The Dieppe summit offers a spectacular view of the surrounding region. Return by the same trail.

Burned Hill

Level of Difficulty:	
Total Distance:	*2.6 km return*
Change in Altitude:	*153 m*
Starting Point:	*Pavillon des Visiteurs (visitor centre).*

There are fifteen information plaques along this short self-guided trail, providing details on the local flora and fauna, as well as the trail's distinctive features. Climb up onto the large boulder at the summit of Burned Hill for a great view. Return by the same trail.

■ **Other Hikes, Walks and Discoveries in the Montérégie Region**

● Mont Rigaud; the trails are presently being rearranged, opening expected for late 1994; information, ☎ (514) 451-0823

● Parc Régional des Îles de Saint-Thimothée; walking, beautiful beach, water sports , ☎ (514) 377-1117

● Mont Saint-Grégoire; beautiful trail, great views; Centre d'Interprétation du Milieu Écologique, ecological information centre, ☎ (514) 346-0406

● Centre d'Interprétation de la Pomme du Québec (Québec apple information centre), in Rougemont; tours, games, ☎ (514) 469-3600

Estrie (The Eastern Townships)

Perhaps one of the most beautiful in Québec, the Estrie, or Eastern Townships region is located in the southernmost part of the province, in the foothills of the Appalachian Mountains. Its rich architectural heritage and hilly terrain create a quaint country feeling reminiscent of small New England towns. Between rolling valleys and rounded mountain tops lie picturesque villages characterized by their distinctly Anglo-Saxon architecture.

Located about one hour's drive from Montréal, the region has become a very popular vacation spot. Winter snow makes for great skiing, and warm summer temperatures fill the lakes and rivers with aquatic enthusiasts of all kinds. People also come to Estrie for its delicious food, the beautiful wine roads, numerous festivals and family activities.

■ Parc Sutton

The Parc d'Environnement Naturel de Sutton covers part of the massif of Mont Sutton. There are 24 km of maintained trails, and a map is offered to visitors. The most popular hike is the one leading to the summit of **Roundtop**, from which the view is spectacular.

In the fall, the park organizes a festival of colours known as the "Panoramaduodlacôte", during which recreational, educational, cultural and sporting activities are offered.

Access: Highway 10, Exit 68. Route 139 South to Sutton, then left on Chemin Maples towards the Mont-Sutton Ski Centre. Turn left again onto Chemin Harold Boulanger, which becomes Chemin Réal, to ALT 540 parking lot. ☎ (514) 538-2646, 538-2339

Roundtop

Level of Difficulty:	◪◪
Total Distance:	*4.6 km return*
Change in Altitude:	*420 m*
Starting Point:	*ALT 540*

This hike includes a number of stunning viewpoints. The trail climbs up to ALT 670 then up to ALT 750, where it meets the Sentiers de l'Estrie (SE, Eastern Townships Trails). The route continues up to

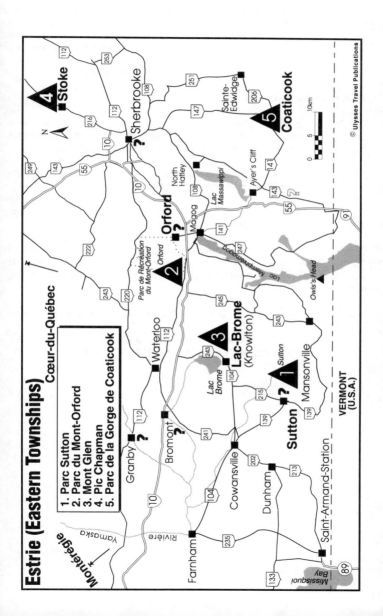

Estrie (Eastern Townships)

1. Parc Sutton
2. Parc du Mont-Orford
3. Mont Glen
4. Pic Chapman
5. Parc de la Gorge de Coaticook

Montérégie

Cœur-du-Québec

© Ulysses Travel Publications

VERMONT (U.S.A.)

ALT 860, where a right turn leads up to the summit of Roundtop, which at 962 m, is the highest point of the Sutton Mountains. The exceptional view stretches from the valley of the Rivière Missisquoi to Jay Peak. Around the viewpoint are various plaques to help visitors identify the neighbouring peaks. Roundtop has subalpine vegetation and bare, rocky outcroppings. Return by the same trail.

■ **Parc du Mont-Orford**

Parc du Mont Orford offers close to 60 km of trails for the exclusive use of hikers and walkers. From short walks to veritable treks (along the Sentiers de l'Estrie), there is certainly no lack of choice.

The two trails described below include the higher part of the superb network of trails known as the Sentiers de l'Estrie (SE).

The park also offers a whole slew of activities, including swimming, sailing, golf, nature interpretation and music.

Parc du Mont Orford was officially declared a recreational park in 1979, but activities have been organized here ever since 1938. It should also be noted that nearly 200 species of birds frequent the park.

Access: Highway 10, Exit 118. Route 141 to the park entrance.

Parc du Mont-Orford ☎ (819) 843-6233
Sentiers de l'Estrie (SE) ☎ (819) 829-1992

Mont Chauve (Sentiers de l'Estrie)

Level of Difficulty:	⌃⌃
Total Distance:	*9 km return*
Change in Altitude:	*300 m*
Starting Point:	*the sign for "Sentiers de l'Estrie" on Route 220, near Chemin Nénuphar, to the north of the park.*

The name of this trail translates literally as "Bald Peak." The trail heads south toward the interior of Parc du Mont Orford. After 1 km, it intersects with the trail for the Auberge La Samarre, then begins to climb gradually up to the intersection with the trail to the northern side of Mont Chauve. Follow the trail to the right to the summit of Mont Chauve (600 m) for a magnificent view. Lac Stukely, the beach and the campground are visible below. In the distance it is possible to make out the Montérégiennes hills, Lac Bowker and the Base de Plein Air Jouvence (outdoor activities station). Return by the same trail.

Variation: On the return trip from the summit of Mont Chauve, you can continue on the Sentiers de l'Estrie trail to the intersection with the trail leading to the summit of the Colline des Sorbiers (580 m), where two great lookout points await. Return by the same trail. This variation adds 2.4 km to the total.

Mont Orford (Sentiers de l'Estrie)

Level of Difficulty:	⌃⌃
Total Distance:	*11.6 km return*
Change in Altitude:	*553 m*
Starting Point:	*sign for "Sentiers de l'Estrie" on Route 112, direction Eastman (1.5 km from Highway 10, Exit 115), south of the park.*

The trail climbs gradually to the rustic campground known as "L'Entremont", then continues until it intersects first with a trail leading to the summit of Mont Giroux, and then, 300 m farther, with another trail which continues to the summit of Mont Orford (853 m).

The view from the summit is spectacular: Mont Chauve to the north, Lac Magog and Mont Chapman to the east, the town of Magog and the Sutton Mountains to the south, and finally Lac Orford to the west! Return by the same trail.

Variation: On the way back, you can take a detour in order to explore the summit of Mont Giroux (624 m), which also has a beautiful, sweeping view. This variation adds 1 km to the total.

■ **Mont Glen**

Mont Glen is located close to Lac Brome (Knowlton). A ski resort in the winter, Mont Glen is just one more reason for hikers to visit and discover the wonders of the Estrie region in the summer. The trail described below is maintained by members of the Sentiers de l'Estrie (SE).

Access: Highway 10, Exit 90. Route 243 South to Lac-Brome (Knowlton). Continue to Chemin Bolton-Glen. Turn left to the parking of the Mont-Glen ski resort.
Sentiers de l'Estrie ☎ (819) 829-1992

Mont Glen (Sentiers de l'Estrie)

Level of Difficulty:	🏔🏔
Total Distance:	*8.4 km return*
Change in Altitude:	*275 m*
Starting Point:	*parking lot of the Mont-Glen ski resort.*

The trail begins at the end of the parking lot. From there it heads downhill to the *poste d'enregistrement* (registration centre, SE). A bit farther along, you will come across a small lookout and then a campground. Beyond this the trail becomes steeper, up to the summit of Mont Glen (590 m), which offers a spectacular view. For an even wider view of the surrounding countryside, walk about 200 m farther. Return by the same trail.

Variation: A beautiful crossing from the Mont Glen ski resort to the rest area on Route 243 is a possible variation on this trail. You will need two cars to complete the trip though, one at the ski centre and one at the rest area. The hike is 11.9 km long and includes some great views of "Bolton Pass" (for information: Sentiers de l'Estrie ☎ 819-829-1992).

■ **Pic Chapman**

This small bare summit is located near the village of Stoke, north of Sherbrooke. The trail leading up to it is part of the Sentiers de l'Estrie

(SE) trail network. It is not, however, part of the long linear hiking trail that links Kingsbury to the American border in northern Vermont.

Access: Highway 10, then Route 216 North towards Stoke. Beyond Stoke, follow Rang XIV to the Sentiers de l'Estrie parking lot.

Pic Chapman (Sentiers de l'Estrie)

Level of Difficulty:	
Total Distance:	*5.6 km return*
Change in Altitude:	*237 m*
Starting Point:	*parking lot, Rang XIV.*

The trail passes by the large Sentiers de l'Estrie (SE) direction indicator, then comes upon a rest area. It starts uphill very gradually at first before becoming quite steep. At the intersection take the left-hand trail to the summit of Pic Chapman (625 m). The spectacular view opens up in every direction and includes Mont Orford, Mont Chauve, Mont Ham and Mont Mégantic. Return by the same trail.

■ Parc de la Gorge de Coaticook

The Gorge de Coaticook is a spectacular natural phenomenon. Measuring 750 m in length, with 50 m-high walls, the gorge has been carved by the tumultuous waters of the Rivière Coaticook.

Well laid-out and maintained, with beautiful short trails, the park is particularly popular with children. Information pannels lead hikers through a whole range of discoveries.

Access :   Highway 10, then Highway 55 toward the United States. Exit at Ayer's Cliff. Route 141 to Coaticook. The entrance to the park is on Rue Michaud.
☎ (819) 849-2331, 849-6669

Tour du Parc

Level of Difficulty:
Total Distance: *3 km loop*
Change in Altitude: *50 m*
Starting Point: *Accueil (visitor centre).*

This easy and pleasant trail leads past the principle attractions of the park, including, of course, the pièce de résistance, the suspended footbridge. Hanging 50 m above the gorge, and measuring 169 m in length, it is the longest suspended footbridge in the world! An observation tower and various lookout points make it possible to view the area as a whole.

■ **Other Hikes, Walks and Discoveries in the Estrie (Eastern Townships) Region**

● Visit the beautiful abbey of Saint-Benoît-du-Lac; cheese and apple cider are sold on the premises, ☎ (819) 843-4080

● Centre d'Interprétation de la Nature du Lac Boivin (Nature Centre), near Granby, ☎ (514) 375-3861

● Parc de Récréation de la Yamaska, northeast of Granby; hiking trails, beach, water sports, ☎ (514) 372-3204

● Parc de Récréation de Frontenac, to the northeast of the Eastern Townships; hiking trails, swimming, canoeing, camping, ☎ (418) 422-2136

● Observatoire de Mont Mégantic, observatory, ☎ (819) 888-2822, and the trails of Mont Mégantic, ☎ (819) 888-2800

● Visit the Cristal Kébec Mines, in Bonsecours; superb quartz crystals; guided visits, centre d'interprétation (information centre), ☎ (514) 535-6550

● The Wine Route; guided tours and wine-tastings in various regional vineyards; information at the Maison Régionale du Tourisme de l'Estrie (regional tourism office), ☎ 1-800-263-1068 or (514) 375-8774

The Laurentides

Undoubtedly the most popular vacation spot in Québec, the beautiful Laurentides region attracts countless visitors every season of the year. People have been heading "up north" for many years to relax and enjoy the natural beauty of the countryside. The numerous lakes mountains and forests provide the perfect setting for countless sports and walks. The Laurentides contain the highest concentration of ski centres in North America, so it is no surprise that with the arrival of winter, skiing is the main attraction. The small villages nestled at the foot of the mountains are quaint and picturesque and well worth exploring.

■ Parc d'Oka

The Parc d'Oka, only 50 km from Montreal, offers easy, well-maintained trails. It is the ideal spot to learn about the natural environment, as many trails are self-guided and provide a wealth of information.

Even though the park is quite small (24 km²), the terrain is extremely varied: hills, fields, marshes, beach, lake, etc.

Access :   Highway 13 or 15 North, then Highway 640 Ouest to the end. Beyond the set of lights, the road leads into Parc d'Oka.
☎(514) 479-8365, 479-8337

Sentier Historique du Calvaire d'Oka

Level of Difficulty:	⌃
Total Distance:	*5.5 km loop*
Change in Altitude:	*100 m*
Starting Point:	*the de l'Orée parking lot.*

The name of this trail translates literally as "Historic Trail of the Oka Calvary." The Calvaire is a small summit measuring 152 m, which offers spectacular views of Lac-des-Deux-Montagnes and the village of Oka as well as the park. This historic trail is in fact a *chemin de croix* (way of the cross), along which can be found four oratories and three chapels constructed between 1740 and 1742 by the fathers of Saint-Sulpice.

There is a shorter route up to the summit of the Calvaire. A trail leading from the parking lot to the summit (the chapels) takes twenty minutes.

Rivière-aux-Serpents

Level of Difficulty:	⌃⌄
Total Distance:	*1.8 km return*
Change in Altitude:	*nil*
Starting Point:	*parking lot of the campground's common room*

This is a short, picturesque trail that leads to the Rivière-aux-Serpents, which is located in a beautiful marshfield. Return by the same trail.

Sentier Écologique de la Grande-Baie

Level of Difficulty:	⌃⌄
Total Distance:	*3 km loop*
Change in Altitude:	*35 m*
Starting Point:	*parking lot of the Centre d'Acceuil et d'Interprétation (visitor information centre).*

This beautiful ecological trail was completely overhauled two years ago. At the beginning of the trail, a small helpful guide book of the trail's highlights is offered free of charge. It provides commentary and information at the various stations along the way.

Within a few short minutes, the trail leads through four ecosystems: a field, a silver maple grove, a caryer maple grove and a marsh. A small floating footbridge and an observation tower, from which the view of the Grande-Baie area is exceptional, can be found in the marsh. This is the ideal spot to catch a glimpse of one of the 200 species of birds that frequent the park.

■ Parc du Mont-Tremblant

Parc du Mont Tremblant has been a recreational park since 1981. Hunting is now forbidden here. With an area of 1,248 km², the park contains more than 400 km of recreational trails for walking, hiking and biking. Mont Tremblant, the mountain, is 968 m high and occupies the western end of the park. This "trembling" mountain was named *Manitonga Soutana* (mountain of spirits or of the Devil) by Algonquin sorcerers after they heard rumbling sounds coming from it. You will have plenty of company on your hikes through the park; 193 species of birds have been counted so far, and there are more and

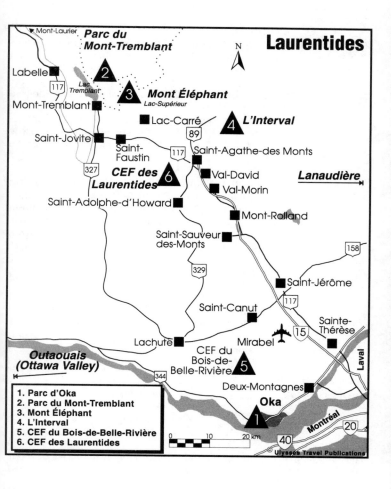

Laurentides

Mont-Laurier

Parc du Mont-Tremblant

Labelle

117
Lac Tremblant

Mont-Tremblant

Saint-Jovite

327

Saint-Faustin

2

3

Mont Éléphant
Lac-Supérieur

Lac-Carré

89

117

4 L'Interval

Saint-Agathe-des Monts

Lanaudière

CEF des Laurentides 6

Val-David

Val-Morin

Saint-Adolphe-d'Howard

Mont-Rolland

Saint-Sauveur des-Monts

329

158

Saint-Jérôme

117

Saint-Canut

Lachute

Outaouais
(Ottawa Valley)

344

CEF du Bois-de-Belle-Rivière 5

Mirabel

15

Sainte-Thérèse

Laval

Deux-Montagnes

Oka 1

Montréal

20

40

1. Parc d'Oka
2. Parc du Mont-Tremblant
3. Mont Éléphant
4. L'Interval
5. CEF du Bois-de-Belle-Rivière
6. CEF des Laurentides

0   10   20 km

© Ulysses Travel Publications

more animals all the time. In the fall it is quite common to see a moose drinking from one of the 500 lakes and rivers within the park! And of course the tireless raccoon will make sure to remind you never to leave food inside your tent.

Besides the short hiking and self-guided trails, there is also a long hike (85 km) with overnights in a shelter. Take note that camping is not permitted in the "Pimbina" and "La Diable" sectors.

Access: To reach the Centre Communautaire du Lac Monroe (community centre), go beyond the Centre d'Accueil La Diable (visitor centre) : Highway 15 North, which becomes Route 117, to Saint-Faustin. From there follow the signs for "Parc du Mont-Tremblant, Secteur La Diable."

To reach the Centre d'Accueil Saint-Donat (visitor centre) : Highway 15 to Sainte-Agathe-des-Monts, then Exit 89 onto Route 329 Est toward Saint-Donat. From there follow the sign for "Centre d'Accueil Saint-Donat du Parc du Mont-Tremblant." Alternate route from Montréal: Highway 25 then Route 125 to Saint-Donat.

Centre d'Accueil La Diable ☎ (819) 688-2281
Centre d'Accueil Saint-Donat ☎ (819) 424-2954
Services Récréatifs Le Boulé (shelters) ☎ 1-800-567-6177
Parc du Mont-Tremblant ☎ (819) 688-2336

La Roche et la Corniche

Level of Difficulty:	
Total Distance:	*8 km loop*
Change in Altitude:	*250 m*
Starting Point:	*Centre Communautaire du Lac Monroe (community centre).*

This loop is pleasant and easy, and offers some lovely views of Mont Tremblant, Lac Monroe and the valley of La Diable. Return by the road along Lac Monroe.

Variation: There are quite a few possiblities with this trail; hike to the lookout point of the La Roche trail (6 km return) or only to the lookout point of the La Corniche trail (3.2 km return). You can also park one car at the La Corniche lot and hike the 6.3 km to the Centre Communautaire du Lac Monroe (community centre).

Lac des Femmes

Level of Difficulty:	
Total Distance:	*2.7 km loop*
Change in Altitude:	*60 m*
Starting Point:	*Centre Communautaire du Lac Monroe (community centre).*

This self-guided nature trail can be hiked in an hour and a half. Rushing through at that rate, however, is not the point — take the time to stop at the 14 information points and read the guide that can be borrowed from the centre.

Curious hikers can thus learn some of the secrest of the Laurentides mountain chain, with its coniferous forests, birch trees, glacial lakes and streams!

You may even get lucky and see one of the seven Québec species of woodpeckers, and if you do not see any keep your ears tuned for the unmistakable "tock-tock-tock!"

Lac aux Atocas

Level of Difficulty:	
Total Distance:	*1.5 km loop*
Change in Altitude:	*30 m*
Starting Point:	*parking lot of the Lac aux Atocas trail, on Route 1, south of the Centre Communautaire du Lac Monroe (community centre).*

This small loop takes less than an hour, and introduces the hiker to different aquatic milieus (lake, river, peat bog and marsh). The balance of these systems is very fragile, so be careful to stick to the trail. There are twelve information stops along the way.

L'Envol

Level of Difficulty:

Total Distance :   *3.6 km return*
Change in Altitude: *215 m*
Starting Point: *Centre d'Accueil Saint-Donat (visitor centre).*

This self-guided nature trail, with twelve information stops along the way, will answer all your questions regarding the life of a yellow birch grove. After this hike the changing fall colours will no longer be one of life's little mysteries! Besides the trees, hikers will also be enlightened by the various animals who make their homes in and around the grove (marten, porcupine, black bear, etc.)

At the summit of l'Envol is a beautiful lookout point. This makes an ideal picnic spot, complete with tables and toilets. Return by the same trail.

Variation: It is possible to return by a different trail, either L'Érablière (which eventually joins L'Envol); or Le Ruisseau, which leads right to the road. These variations do not alter the total distance.

La Pimbina

Level of Difficulty:

Total Distance: *28.2 km one way only*
Change in Altitude: *425 m*
Starting Point: *the Chute aux Rats parking lot, north of the Centre d'Accueil Saint-Donat (visitor centre). Reservations (shelters) and information ☎ 1-800-567-6177.*

This straight one-way trail is 28.2 km long and takes two days of walking with one overnight in the shelter at Lac des Sables (camping is not permitted). The trail ends up at the Chutes Croches (crooked falls) parking lot on Route 1 (two cars required).

Day one (13 km) involves a few challenging uphill climbs, two spectacular viewpoints, and a downhill stretch to the shelter at Lac des Sables.

Day Two (15.2 km) also includes a beautiful panoramic view. The trail then leads to the south of Lac Escalier and skirts round Lac Ernie before heading down to Route 1.

Variation: This hike can be lengthened to three days and two nights by continuing on to the Centre Communautaire du Lac Monroe (35.2 km); overnight the second night in the shelter at Lac Ernie (day 1 = 13 km, day 2 = 9.6 km, day 3 = 12.6 km).

La Diable

Level of Difficulty:	⛰️⛰️
Total Distance:	*45 km loop*
Change in Altitude:	*250 m*
Starting Point:	*Centre Communautaire du Lac Monroe (community centre) parking lot. Reservations (shelters) and information ☎ 1-800-567-6177.*

This 45 km hike takes three days and two nights; day 1 = 18.6 km, day 2 = 15.6 km, day 3 = 10.8 km.

The loop can be hiked in one direction or the other. The clockwise route is less difficult, however, since the longest hike (18.6 km) comes on the first day, when most hikers will be in better form.

Day 1 (18.6 km): Although the change in altitude is negligeable, the total distance for the day is quite substantial. There is a beautiful view close to Rivière Cachée. Overnight at the La Cache shelter.

Day 2 (15.6 km): After skirting Lac Caché, the trail leads to three lookout points, then passes close to the Lac Croche dam before reaching the Le Liteau shelter.

Day 3 (10.8 km): From the shelter the trail heads down toward the Chutes Croches, then branches off toward the Centre Communautaire du Lac Monroe (community centre).

Variation: It is possible to hike the Pimbina and Diable trails one after the other. This is a 64.8 km trip, which takes five days (with four overnights in shelters).

■ Mont Éléphant

Mont Éléphant is located to the northwest of Lac Supérieur, between the village of the same name and Parc du Mont-Tremblant (La Diable sector). It offers a great hike for the whole family, dotted with beautiful views of the valley.

Access: Highway 15, Route 117 to Saint-Faustin. Then head towards Parc du Mont-Tremblant, all the way to the Auberge du Versant-Nord (north-side chalet), (☎ 819-688-3355).

Mont Éléphant

Level of Difficulty:	⌂
Total Distance:	*7 km loop*
Change in Altitude:	*240 m*
Starting Point:	*Auberge du Versant-Nord.*

The owner of the Auberge du Versant-Nord is very friendly and will let hikers park free of charge. The trail climbs gradually all the way to the summit of Mont Éléphant (575 m), which offers a truly stunning view out over the Laurentides and Lac Supérieur. From the summit the trail heads down to Chemin du Lac Supérieur, which leads back to the Auberge. Mont Éléphant is so named because it is said to resemble a sleeping elephant when viewed from the village of Lac-Supérieur.

Variation: For a shorter hike, retrace your steps once you have reached the summit.

■ L'Interval

L'Interval is the name of an Auberge de Plein Air (backwoods inn and outdoor centre) located in Sainte-Lucie-des-Laurentides, on the shores of Lac Legault.

The trails were originally cleared for cross-country skiers, but they remain popular year-round. There are nine marked trails to choose from, covering a total distance of 45 km. The best hike is without a doubt along the trail leading to the summit of Mont Kaaikop (830 m). The Auberge provides a trail map. If you are not staying at the Auberge you must pay for parking.

Access: Auberge de Plein Air L'Interval. Highway 15, Exit 89. Route 329 for 19 km. After Lac Creux, turn right and follow the signs.
☎ (819) 326-4069

Mont Legault

Level of Difficulty:
Total Distance: *6 km return*
Change in Altitude: *330 m*
Starting Point: *Auberge L'Interval.*

The Mont Legault trail leads to the summit of Mont Kaaikop (830 m), which used to be called Mont Legault, since the mountain is located near the lake of the same name. Kaaikop means "high, steep and rocky place."

The hike up is short but also steep, and therefore quite difficult. The last 100 metres are steeper still, and very demanding. Keep pushing, though, because the view from the summit is one of the most spectacular in the Laurentides. Return by the same trail.

Variation: The Mont Legault trail is actually an 11.8 km loop. The trail is not marked as clearly in summer as it is in winter, and hikers must be careful not to stray off it.

Tour du Lac

Level of Difficulty :
Total Distance: *3.3 km loop*
Change in Altitude: *60 m*
Starting Point: *Auberge L'Interval.*

This is an easy but beautiful short loop that skirts the shores of Lac Legault.

L'Érablière

Level of Difficulty:	⛰
Total Distance:	*4.4 km loop*
Change in Altitude:	*80 m*
Starting Point:	*Auberge L'Interval.*

This trail, to the southeast of Lac Legault, is very easy and winds through a forest, which is particularly beautiful in the fall.

■ **CEF du Bois-de-Belle-Rivière**

This Centre Éducatif Forestier (CEF, Forestry Education Centre), 65 km from Montréal near Mirabel, occupies a magnificent carver maple grove. Undergrowth, thick forest, decorative gardens, and an orchard adorn the surroundings. There are five different hikes covering eight kilometres of trail; the two most interesting are L'Érablière (3.7 km loop) and Le Sylvestre (1.8 km loop). At press time the centre was closed. At press time the centre was closed. It is expected to reopen under new management soon, but be sure to call ahead first.

Access: Highway 15, Exit 35. Follow Boulevard Mirabel, then Route 148 Est.
☎ (514) 258-3433, 1-800-363-2589 (from Montréal)

■ **CEF des Laurentides**

The CEF (Forestry Education Centre) des Laurentides, located between Sainte-Agathe-des-Monts and Saint-Faustin, spreads over rough terrain covered with lakes and mountains (laurentian maple grove). Magnificent little footbridges complement some of the trails. There are 14.7 km of trails (four self-guided nature trails and two hiking trails). The Panoramique trail (3 km return) leads up to the summit of a small mountain (460 m), where hikers can enjoy a magnificent view. The centre was closed in April of 1994, but was reopened under new management in June.

Access :   Highway 15, Exit 83. Chemin des Lacs, then Chemin du Lac-Caribou.
☎ (819) 326-1606

■ **Other Hikes, Walks and Discoveries in the Laurentides Region**

● Centre d'Interprétation de la Nature de Boisbriand; picturesque hiking trails, ☎ (514) 437-2727

● Parc du Domaine Vert, near Blainville; hiking, swimming, horseback riding, ☎ (514) 435-6510

● Parc Régional de la Rivière-du-Nord, north of Saint-Jérôme, ☎ (514) 431-1676

● Parc de la Rivière-Doncaster, in Mont-Rolland, ☎ (514) 229-2200

● Val-David; hiking through Mont Césaire, Mont Condor and Mont King; rock-climbing centre of Québec

● Réserve Faunique de Papineau-Labelle (provincial wildlife reserve), ☎ (819) 771-4840

● The Petit Castor ecological trail, at Lac-du-Cerf; 2.8 km self-guided trial, well maintained, ☎ (819) 597-2424

● Chute du Windigo (waterfall) and Mont Sir-Wilfrid (783 m) near Ferme-Neuve

Lanaudière

The Lanaudière region spreads out immediately to the north of Montréal, from the St-Laurent plain to the beginning of the Laurentian plateau. Except for that section which is a part of the metropolitan region, the Lanaudière region consists of calm lakes and rivers, farmland, wild forests and great open spaces.

■ **Chertsey**

The Grande Vallée sector, near Chertsey exists thanks to the relentless efforts of volunteers, especially Paul Perrault, who conceived the project.

It all began in 1964, when Paul Perrault and his son decided to cut a trail linking a few of the lakes in the valley. Over the years this linear trail grew longer, reaching 14 km in 1984. Other trails were added to it, creating a network of trails, that today covers 30 km.

Well laid-out and well marked, the Grande Vallée trails come in all levels of difficulty, and therefore have something to offer everyone in the family, as well as serious trekkers. Magnificent, secluded little lakes and endless panoramic views await.

Access: Route 125 North to Chertsey, then Rue de l'Église and Boulevard Grande-Vallée.
☎ (514) 882-1558

Le Sommet

Level of Difficulty:	⌂
Total Distance:	*7 km return*
Change in Altitude:	*300 m*
Starting Point:	*parking lot on Rue des Pâquerettes.*

This is a relatively easy trail leading to the peak known as Le Sommet (540 m). There are two beautiful lookout points along the way. From the parking lot follow the Grande Vallée trail for 2.7 km (a long uphill climb) to the intersection with the Sommet trail, and head toward the summit. The trail becomes increasingly steep up to the summit. Return by the same trail.

Variation: You can continue on the trail down the other side (northeast) of the mountain, which leads to Boulevard Grande-Vallée then back to Rue des Pâquerettes, making a loop of about 10 km.

Mt-107

Level of Difficulty:	⌂ ⌂
Total Distance:	*7.4 km return*
Change in Altitude:	*380 m*
Starting Point:	*Boulevard Grande-Vallée, parking lot near the sign for Mt-107.*

The starting point is located almost at the end of Boulevard Grande-Vallée. Be careful, particularly in the spring, as this section of the road is often scarred with potholes. It is 3.7 km to the summit, and the trail is quite difficult, leading straight up the mountainside, with a significant change in altitude. The reward comes at the summit though, with a truly breathtaking view. On a clear day it stretches all the way to Montréal. Return by the same trail.

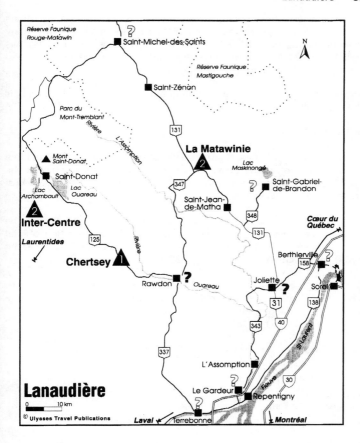

Grande Vallée

Level of Difficulty:	⌃⌃
Total Distance:	*13.5 km one-way only*
Change in Altitude:	*250 m*
Starting Point:	*parking lot on Rue des Pâquerettes.*

This linear trail traverses the entire valley. You will therefore need two cars, one at the starting point and the other parked at the beginning of Chemin du Lac Beauregard (5.6 km north of Lac Pauzé, on Route 125).

This trail should not present any difficulties, since the uphill sections are not too steep. Given the length of the trail, there are not very many lookout points, but you will quickly realize that the joy of hiking this trail comes from the peaceful serenity of the surrounding forest and the small pristine lakes along the way.

The beginning of the hike, an unrelenting three-kilometre uphill haul, is the most difficult.

■ La Matawinie

The Matawinie trails near Sainte-Émélie-de-l'Énergie (Lanaudière) have been around for a long time, but were not as well maintained in the past. Recent years have seen great improvements in the network of trails (upkeep, markers, etc.).

Among the various trails in the area is the 12 km linear trail, the "Matawinie", which has the distinct honour of being the first official marked section of the National Trail (Sentier National). This sacred event took place on October 27, 1990.

Access: Highway 40, Exit 122, then Route 31 and 131 North. After Sainte-Émélie-de-l'Énergie, follow Rang 4 to the parking lot.
             ☎ (514) 886-3823

Sentier Matawinie (Sentier National)

Level of Difficulty:	🏔🏔
Total Distance:	*12 km one way*
Change in Altitude:	*200 m*
Starting Point:	*Rang 4 parking lot.*

This linear trail (arrange for two cars) traverses the crest of the mountains alongside the valley of the Rivière Noire, within the borders of the town of Sainte-Émélie-de-l'Énergie.

Various intersections all along the trail provide access to various lakes (Koel, Coutu, etc.) and summits. There are several lookout points, which provide an interesting perspective of the superb Matawinian forest. The trail ends close to the *"mer des montagnes"* (sea of montains), a summit which towers over Lac Coutu. The continuation of the trail to the Sept-Chutes (seven falls) in Saint-Zénon is planned for the near future.

Côte à Monette

Level of Difficulty:	
Total Distance:	*5 km return*
Change in Altitude:	*100 m*
Starting Point:	*parking lot of the Côte à Monette trail, on Route 131, north of Rang 4.*

This short trail is actually only 1 km long, to Lac Koel. Once at the lake, though you can join up with the Matawinie trail heading south, until you reach the "Sentier du Point de Vue" (lookout point trail) which is a short uphill climb. This easy hike is a great way to admire the region. The hike can also be done on snowshoes during winter. Return by the same trail.

Variation: It is possible to make a loop by continuing south on the Matawinie trail to the Rang 4 parking lot then following Route 131 back to the starting point.

■ **Inter-Centre**

The Inter-Centre trail is located close to Parc du Mont-Tremblant and links the towns of Lac-Supérieur and Saint-Donat. As such the trail crosses both the Lanaudière region and the Laurentides region. This linear trail also includes two smaller access trails (at Val-des-Lacs) making one-day hikes possible.

In total there are 40 km of trails, marked and maintained by the *Corporation des Sentiers de Grande Randonnée des Laurentides* (hiking co-op). Two shelters (Le Nordet and L'Appel) are available to hikers (reservations: ☎ 514-389-1942, Normand Sharkey). Take note that the section of trail starting near the Auberge La Boulée has been diverted. From now on you must follow the trails of the Centre d'Accès à la Nature de l'UQAM (UQAM's Nature Centre), which also offers hikers the use of its parking lot.

The Inter-Centre trail is a part of the National Trail (Sentier National). It was inaugurated in October of 1990.

Access: Saint-Donat sector; Highway 15, then Route 329 toward Saint-Donat. South of Lac Archambault, take the road on the left, following the signs for Inter-Centre.

Lac-Supérieur sector; Centre d'Accès à la Nature de l'U-
QAM ☎ (819) 688-3212 or (514) 987-3105. Highway 15, then Route 117 to Saint-Faustin. Head towards
Lac Carré and Parc du Mont-Tremblant. Just before the
town of Lac-Supérieur, follow the road to the right
towards the Auberge La Boulé, 1.6 km down the road.

Inter-Centre; ☎ (514) 389-1942, Normand Sharkey.

Inter-Centre (Montagne Noire)

Level of Difficulty:	🏔🏔
Total Distance:	*14 km return*
Change in Altitude:	*450 m*
Starting Point:	*parking lot south of Lac Archam-* *bault.*

This trail is difficult because it leads continuously uphill, and there are
few chances to relax or take a breather. It does however lead to one
of the most picturesque summits in the Laurentides, the summit of
Montagne Noire (900 m, Black Mountain). The view from the summit
of the valleys, lakes and mountains as well as Lac Archambault is
splendid! It will make you wish you could climb higher! Return by the
same trail.

Inter-Centre (Montagne Grise)

Level of Difficulty:	🏔🏔
Total Distance:	*17 km loop*
Change in Altitude:	*400 m*
Starting Point:	*parking lot of the Centre d'Accès à* *la Nature de l'UQAM.*

The first part of the hike follows trails laid out by of the Centre
d'Accès à la Nature, up to the summit of Montagne Grise (760 m,
Grey Mountain), and a breathtaking view.

From the summit of Montagne Grise, the trail heads down to the
Nordet shelter. From there, follow the Inter-Centre trail west along the
side of Montagne Grise to return to the Centre d'Accès à la Nature.
Some great lookout points provide superb views of Mont Tremblant,
Mont Nixon and Mont Éléphant

The Centre d'Accès à la Nature de l'UQAM offers many other beautiful hiking trails, as well as accommodation (for information: ☎ 514-987-3105).

Inter-Centre

Level of Difficulty:	◪◪◪
Total Distance:	*30 km one-way only*
Change in Altitude:	*450 m*
Starting Point:	*parking lot south of Lac Archambault and at the Centre d'Accès à la Nature de l'UQAM. Arrange for two cars.*

This hike takes two days (overnight at the Lac l'Appel shelter).

Day 1 (14 km): From the parking lot at Lac Archambault, the trail is very steep all the way to the summit of Montagne Noire (900 m), from which the view is magnificent. The trail then descends to Lac Raquette, before heading uphill for a bit to reach the Lac l'Appel shelter.

Day 2 (16 km): From the shelter at Lac de l'Appel, the trail slowly descends to an intersection. Head toward the Nordet shelter, where the trail follows the crest of Montagne Grise and offers a fantastic view of the neighbouring summits, including the beautiful Mont Tremblant. The trail then heads down to the parking lot at the Centre d'Accès à la Nature de l'UQAM, where your second car should be parked.

■ Other Hikes, Walks and Discoveries in the Lanaudière Region

● Parc des Chutes-Dorwin, in Rawdon, ☎ (514) 834-2151

● Parc Régional des Chutes-Monte-à-Peine-et-des-Dalles, near Saint-Jean-de-Matha, ☎ (514) 883-2245 et 886-9114

● Sept-Chutes observation deck, in Saint-Zénon; beautiful trails including a self-guided nature trail, ☎ (514) 884-5437

● Sainte-Geneviève-de-Berthier, near Berthierville; nature interpretation trails (5 km), ☎ 836-7845, 836-6758

- The Jardin Forestier à Saint-Charles-de-Mandeville; more than 500 sculpted trees, some in the shape of animals, ☎ (514) 835-1377

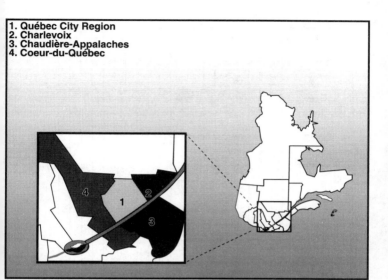

1. Québec City Region
2. Charlevoix
3. Chaudière-Appalaches
4. Coeur-du-Québec

QUÉBEC CITY AND REGION

Q uébec City stands out as much for the outstanding richness of its architectural heritage as for the beauty of its location. A picturesque region of open country and mountains lies within close proximity of the provincial capital.

This chapter covers the tourist regions of Québec City, Charlevoix, Chaudières-Appalaches and Cœur-du-Québec.

Québec City

The Haute-Ville (Upper Town) of Québec City is located on a 98 m-high promontory called **Cap aux Diamant** (Cape Diamond), overhanging the Fleuve St-Laurent, where it narrows to a mere one kilometre. In fact, it is this narrowing of the river that gives the city its name: in Algonquian, *kebec* means "place where the river narrows." The heights of Cap aux Diamant dominate the river and surrounding countryside and offer a spectacular view. From the early days of New France, this

QUÉBEC CITY AND REGION

	Level of Difficulty of Hike	Total Distance of Hike (km)	Change in Altitude (m)	Page
SHORT HIKES				
Réserve Nationale de Faune du Cap Tourmente : La Cédrière	◿	3.1	0	98
Réserve Nationale de Faune du Cap Tourmente : Le Bois-Sent-Bon	◿	2.0	0	99
Réserve Nationale de Faune du Cap Tourmente : La Cime and La Falaise	◿◿	7.5	560	99
Parc de la Jacques-Cartier : l'Aperçu	◿	1.7	60	100
Parc de la Jacques-Cartier : Les Cascades	◿	4.3	90	101
Parc de la Jacques-Cartier : Les Coulées	◿◿	9.7	180	101
Parc de la Jacques-Cartier : Les Loups	◿◿	7.6	473	101
Parc de la Jacques-Cartier : L'Andante	◿◿◿	16.0	465	102
Parc des Grands-Jardins : Le Gros Pin	◿	1.8	30	104
Parc des Grands-Jardins : Mont du Lac des Cygnes	◿◿	5.2	440	104
Parc des Grands-Jardins : Le Boréal	◿	1.9	30	106
Parc des Grands-Jardins : La Pinède	◿	6.0	0	106
Parc des Grands-Jardins : De la Chute	◿	5.0	0	107
Parc des Hautes-Gorges de la Rivière Malbaie : Mont des Érables	◿◿◿	8.8	780	108
Parc des Hautes-Gorges de la Rivière Malbaie : Mont Acropole des Draveurs	◿◿◿	4.2	790	108
Parc des Hautes-Gorges de la Rivière Malbaie : L'Érablière	◿	1.6	minimal	109
Parc des Hautes-Gorges de la Rivière Malbaie : Le Belvédère	◿	1.2	400	109
Parc des Hautes-Gorges de la Rivière Malbaie : Chutes du Ruisseau Blanc	◿	2.2	minimal	109
Parc des Hautes-Gorges de la Rivière Malbaie : Chutes du Lac Scott	◿	2.2	minimal	109

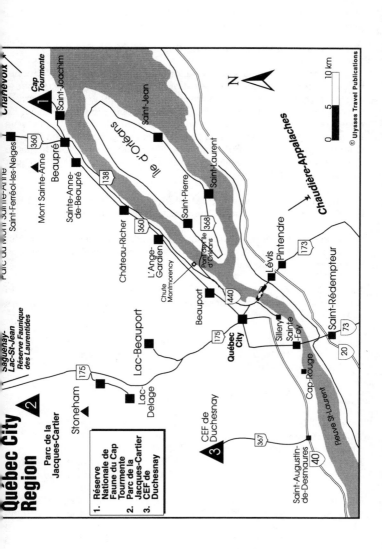

Québec City Region

Parc de la Jacques-Cartier

1. Réserve Nationale de Faune du Cap Tourmente
2. Parc de la Jacques-Cartier
3. CEF de Duchesnay

Saguenay-Lac-St-Jean
Réserve Faunique des Laurentides

Charlevoix

Cap Tourmente

Saint-Joachim

Beaupré

Mont Sainte-Anne

Sainte-Anne-de-Beaupré

Château-Richer

L'Ange-Gardien

Chute Montmorency

Beauport

Québec City

Île d'Orléans

Saint-Jean

Saint-Laurent

Saint-Pierre

Pont de l'Île d'Orléans

Lévis

Pintendre

Chaudière-Appalaches

Saint-Rédempteur

Sillery

Sainte-Foy

Cap-Rouge

Fleuve St-Laurent

Saint-Augustin-de-Desmaures

CEF de Duchesnay

Lac-Beauport

Lac-Delage

Stoneham

N

0   5   10 km

© Ulysses Travel Publications

rocky peak played an important strategic role and quickly became the site of major fortifications. Dubbed the "Gibraltar of North America", today Québec City is the only walled city north of Mexico.

■ Réserve Nationale de Faune du Cap Tourmente

The Réserve Nationale de Faune du Cap Tourmente is a national wildlife reserve located 50 km east of Québec City on the north shore of the St-Laurent. The reserve was created in 1969 in order to protect the bulrush marsh, the habitat of the only population of great white geese (also know as snow geese) in the world. In 1981 the reserve became the first Canadian area given world recognition by the Ramsar Convention. The population of great white geese has thrived thanks to the protection it has received, increasing from 89,000 in 1970, to over 300,000 in 1986!

It is possible to observe the great white geese in both spring and fall, but the best period is during the first two weeks of October.

Geese are not the only inhabitants of the reserve; 250 species of birds, 45 species of mammals and 700 species of plants will also keep you company on your outings!

As for hiking, the reserve maintains a network of 18 km (ten trails in total). Cap Tourmente, a cape, rises up 571 m. The reserve offers guided trails, audiovisual presentations and exhibitions.

Access: from Québec City, Route 138 to Beaupré. Then Route 360 to St-Joachim and Cap Tourmente.
              ☎ (418) 827-4591, 827-3776

         La Cédrière

Level of Difficulty: ⌂
Total Distance: *3.1 km loop*
Change in Altitude: *nil*
Starting Point: *Centre d'Interprétation Faunique (wildlife information centre).*

This trail leads first to a cultivated prairie then through the *cédrière*, or cedar grove near the cliff, before heading down to the pond for a glimpse of all the activity taking place there. You might even spot a peregrine falcon around the cliff! This endangered animal species has only recently been reintroduced to the area.

Le Bois-Sent-Bon

Level of Difficulty:	⌂
Total Distance:	*2 km loop*
Change in Altitude:	*nil*
Starting Point:	*Centre d'Interprétation Faunique (wildlife information centre).*

The name of this trail translates literally as "the forest smells good." It leads to the edge of a marsh along the shores of the Fleuve St-Laurent where the great white geese stop over to rest and replenish their nutritional reserves. These birds travel 6,000 km! The trail passes by a wonderfully aromatic wooded area and then runs alongside a stream that is flooded twice a day by the tide.

La Cime and La Falaise

Level of Difficulty:	⌂⌂
Total Distance:	*7.5 km return*
Change in Altitude:	*560 m*
Starting Point:	*Centre d'Interprétation Faunique (wildlife information centre).*

The names of these trails translate literally as "the peak" and "the cliff." The La Cime trail leads to the peak of Cap Tourmente. It is fairly difficult since it climbs steadily and is quite steep. Though the view from the summit is not spectacular in all directions, the summit itself does however make up for your efforts, thanks to the fairly dense vegetation. On the way down be sure to check out the view from La Falaise, or the cliff, along the trail of the same name. The panoramic view from here is fantastic. The river, plain and marsh become one. Return by the same trail.

Variation: For a shorter hike, it is possible to take only the La Falaise trail, for a total of 4.3 km return.

■ **Parc de la Jacques-Cartier**

Located just 40 km north of Québec City, in the Québec City tourist region, Parc de la Jacques-Cartier is a treat for both eyes and ears.

Half the park is made up of a narrow valley, 500 m deep, the Vallée de la Jacques-Cartier, through which flows the magnificent Rivière

Jacques-Cartier; while the other half consists of a vast plateau covered by the most northern type of forest in the world, the Boreal forest.

Parc de la Jacques-Cartier saw the light of day in 1981. Before then and since the beginning of the century the park was part of the Parc des Laurentides. With an area if 670 km², it contains a wide variety of wildlife: 132 species of birds and 23 species of mammals, including white-tailed deer, moose, black bears, wolves and lynxes. The park organizes moose safaris — not for hunting, but to see and hear the male react to the call of the female. The park also organizes nocturnal wolf call sessions. These two activities are organized by wildlife specialist, Pierre Vaillancourt (reservations: ☎ 1-800-665-6527).

Very recently, the park reintroduced atlantic salmon into the Rivière Jacques-Cartier. These fish come to spawn in the Rivière Sautauriski in mid-October.

One hundred kilometres of trails are open to hikers. However, of the 14 trails, 6 have to be shared with mountain-bike enthusiasts. It is therefore important to pay close attention since you may be overtaken by a band of fluorescent helmets and lycra at any moment!

Access: from Québec City, the Autoroute Laurentienne 73, then Route 175 to the Secteur de la Vallée entrance.
☎ (418) 848-3169

L'Aperçu

Level of Difficulty:
Total Distance: *1.7 km loop*
Change in Altitude: *60 m*
Starting Point: *parking lot of l'Aperçu or that of the Centre d'Accueil et d'Interprétation (visitor and information centre, 700 m more return).*

The name of this trail translates literally as "the overview." It is a small self-guided trail with a brochure that explains the history of the Vallée de la Jacques-Cartier, and all of the elements that make up the valley. The tour takes less than an hour.

Les Cascades

Level of Difficulty:	◠
Total Distance:	*4.3 km loop*
Change in Altitude:	*90 m*
Starting Point:	*Centre d'Accueil et d'Interprétation (visitor and information centre).*

After crossing the Rivière Jacques-Cartier, follow the Draveur trail to the Cascades trail, which forms a small loop before rejoining the Draveur trail and returning to the starting point. The Cascades trail runs alongside a small stream.

Les Coulées

Level of Difficulty:	◠◠
Total Distance:	*9.7 km loop*
Change in Altitude:	*180 m*
Starting Point:	*Centre d'Accueil et d'Interprétation (visitor and information centre).*

It is best to hike this loop in a counter-clockwise direction. Therefore, start off on the Les Coulées trail, which climbs steeply up to a superb viewpoint. It then heads down gradually to the Rivière Sautauriski. At the intersection here, turn left on the Rivière Sautauriski trail. The trail runs alongside the river, which empties into the Rivière Jacques-Cartier, then follows the road called Chemin du Parc back to the visitor and information centre.

Les Loups

Level of Difficulty:	◠◠
Total Distance:	*7.6 km return*
Change in Altitude:	*473 m*
Starting Point:	*parking lot of the Les Loups trail.*

This trail is definitely one of the most beautiful in the park. The trail climbs considerably (260 m) over the first kilometre and a half. At the intersection, be sure to check out the (550 m) lookout point, or *belvédère* for an exceptional view. The Rivière Jacques-Cartier lies wedged directly below. Retrace your steps a bit for the gradual climb up to the summit of Montagne de la Sautauriski (763 m). The huge crack of the massif as well as the Jacques-Cartier and Sautauriski rivers are visible. Return by the same trail.

L'Andante

Level of Difficulty:	⌂⌂⌂
Total Distance:	*16 km return*
Change in Altitude:	*465 m*
Starting Point:	*parking lot at Le Scotora.*

To reach the Andante (Italian pronunciation) trail, you first have to follow the Scotora trail, which is a considerable trek in itself. It is a historic route, once used by the Jesuits to get to Lac Saint-Jean. They must have had strong muscles, since the trail climbs constantly (almost 400 m over the first five kilometres)! The panoramic view is worth the effort, though. At the intersection, take the Andante trail, which is not as steep, up to the summit of Mont Andante (809 m). The lookout point (755 m) is particularly impressive. Return by the same trail.

■ **CEF de Duchesnay**

The Centre Éducatif Forestier (CEF, Forestry Education Centre) de Duschenay is located on the land of the Station Forestière de Duchesnay (used for research and education), on the shores of Lac Saint-Joseph. Only 45 km northwest of Québec City, it is the ideal spot to get reacquainted with nature and learn a few of the secrets it guards.

There are 14 km of trails: three *sentiers d'interprétation*, or self-guided trails and four hiking trails. The Riverain trail (5.2 km loop) leads to some magnificent lookout points over Lac Saint-Joseph. An educational scavenger hunt rally is also possible along this trail. At press time the centre was closed. It is espected to reopen under new management soon, but be sure to call ahead first.

Access:	Highway 40, Exit 295. Toward Sainte-Catherine-de-la-Jacques-Cartier.
	☎ (418) 875-2711

■ **Other Hikes, Walks and Discoveries in the Québec City Region**

● Stroll through Vieux-Québec, the old part of the city, particularly the Parc des Champs-de-Bataille (Battlefields Park), ☎ (418) 648-4071, and the Fortifications-de-Québec, ☎ (418) 648-7016

- Explore the picturesque villages on Île d'Orléans; pick your own strawberries, apples or corn, ☎ (418) 828-9411

- Hiking in Parc du Mont-Sainte-Anne, ☎ (418) 827-4561

- Hiking at the Station Touristique de Stoneham, ☎ 1-800-463-6888 or (418) 848-2411

- Hiking in the Réserve Faunique de Portneuf; Chutes de la Marmite waterfalls, ☎ (418) 323-2021

- Parc de la Chute-Montmorency; 83 m-waterfall and spectacular foot-bridge, ☎ (418) 663-2877

- Grand Canyon des Chutes Saint-Anne, in Beaupré; 74 m-waterfall, foot-bridge, giant pothole ☎ (418) 827-4057

Charlevoix

Many artists have been captivated by the beauty of the Charlevoix region. From the town of Saint-Joachim to the mouth of the Rivière Saguenay, dramatic mountainous countryside contrasts sharply with the vast expanse of the Fleuve St-Laurent. A scattering of charming villages and towns dot the coastline and its series of narrow valleys and mountains that fall away into the salt water of the river. Away from the river, Charlevoix is a wild, rugged region where Boreal forest sometimes gives way to taiga.

The area's rich architectural heritage and exceptional geography are complemented by a dazzling variety of flora and fauna. The Charlevoix region was named a "World Biosphere Reserve" in 1988 by UNESCO, and is home to many fascinating animal and plant species. Deep in the hinterland, the territory takes on the characteristics of the taiga, an unusual occurrence at this latitude, and is home to animal species such as the caribou and the arctic wolf.

■ Parc des Grands-Jardins

Parc des Grands-Jardins is also known as "Îlôt du Grand Nord Québécois" (Island of Québec's Far North) because it is home to subarctic flora and fauna. Taiga a sparse forest, covers close to a third of the park. A carpet of lichen, northern flowers, dwarf birch trees and black pines make the park look like a giant garden, hence the name Grands-Jardins, which means big gardens.

The park was created in 1981, but had been part of the Parc des Laurentides since 1895.

Over the last few years, caribou-watching has become the park's major attraction. In 1909, the park was home to some 400 caribous, but hunting quickly decimated the population. Less than ten years later, there were none left!

It was not until 1969 that caribou could once again be found in the park. In three years 82 caribous were introduced into the area. By 1985 the population was barely 70 animals, but today there are more than 130.

The park contains seven trails, covering a total of almost 30 km. Guided hikes are also organized.

Access: Route 138, then Route 381 to St-Urbain and the entrance to the park (20 km north of St-Urbain).
☎ (418) 846-2057, 457-3945

Le Gros Pin

Level of difficulty:

Total Distance: *1.8 km loop*
Change in Altitude: *30 m*
Starting Point: *Poste d'Accueil Thomas-Fortin (visitor centre).*

The name of this trail translates literally as "the big pine." This short trail leads through a pretty forest and takes less than an hour to complete. It is the perfect warm-up before attacking Mont du Lac des Cygnes, located just in front.

Mont du Lac des Cygnes

Level of Difficulty:

Total Distance: *5.2 km return*
Change in Altitude: *440 m*
Starting Point: *parking lot of Mont du Lac des Cygnes, located just beyond the Poste d'Accueil Thomas-Fortin (visitor centre) on Route 381.*

Charlevoix

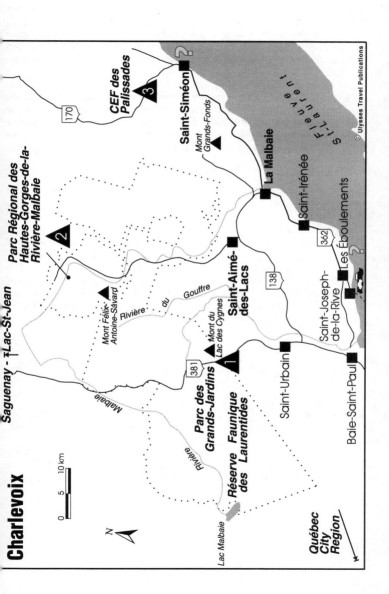

Saguenay - Lac-St-Jean

CEF des Palissades

Saint-Siméon

Parc Régional des Hautes-Gorges-de-la-Rivière-Malbaie

Mont Grands-Fonds

La Malbaie

Saint-Irénée

Les Éboulements

Mont Félix-Antoine-Savard

Rivière du Gouffre

Saint-Aimé-des-Lacs

Saint-Joseph-de-la-Rive

Mont du Lac des Cygnes

Parc des Grands-Jardins

Saint-Urbain

Réserve Faunique des Laurentides

Baie-Saint-Paul

Rivière Malbaie

Lac Malbaie

Québec City Region

0   5   10 km

N

© Ulysses Travel Publications

A *cygne* is a swan. The forest fire that ravaged part of the mountain in May of 1991 hardly marred the beauty of this hike at all. And nature has already reclaimed its position here, as the ground is once again covered with vegetation. One thing is sure: the mesmerizing view from the summit of the mountain over Lac des Cygnes did not go up in smoke!

The trail is not very long; however, the climb to the summit of Mont du Lac des Cygnes is quite steep, gaining more than 400 m over 2.6 km! From the summit (960 m), the view extends over the valley of Baie-Saint-Paul, the Fleuve St-Laurent and the Éboulements, shaped by the impact of a meteorite. Return by the same trail.

Le Boréal

Level of Difficulty:	⌂
Total Distance:	*1.9 km loop*
Change in Altitude:	*30 m*
Starting Point:	*parking lot of the Centre d'Accueil Château-Beaumont (visitor centre).*

On this short self-guided trail, the emphasis is placed on the flora and fauna found in the park, especially the taiga. All information is included in a small brochure, which can be borrowed from the Château-Beaumont visitor centre.

La Pinède

Level of Difficulty:	⌂
Total Distance:	*6 km loop*
Change in Altitude:	*nil*
Starting Point:	*parking lot of the Centre d'Accueil Château-Beaumont (visitor centre).*

This trail crosses a grey pinewood (*pinède*). It is very easy, has no change in altitude, and takes little time. There are beautiful views of the neighbouring lakes and traces of the forest fire can still be seen.

De la Chute

Level of Difficulty:	⌂
Total Distance:	*5 km return*
Change in Altitude:	*nil*
Starting Point:	*the de la Chute parking lot on Route 60, west of the park.*

This trail across the taiga leads to a great lookout point over the superb Rivière Malbaie (which can be explored on canoe-camping trips). At the end of the trail, if you advance far enough, the 15 m-high Chute W. H. Blake (waterfall) is visible. Return by the same trail.

■ **Parc Régional des Hautes-Gorges-de-la-Rivière-Malbaie**

Are you familiar with the Parc Régional des Hautes-Gorges-de-la-Rivière-Malbaie? No? Well, get ready to explore this little gem, and be sure to bring along your camera.

Parc Régional des Hautes-Gorges-de-la-Rivière-Malbaie is still unknown to many, but it is only a matter of time before outdoor enthusiasts take it over. The wild beauty of the Rivière Malbaie being forced between immense rock faces measuring more than 700 m high, is sure to amaze nature lovers!

A deep valley, superb river, spectacular falls, gargantuan walls of rock and high peaks make this park a hallowed place for outdoor activities in Québec. The rush of activity continues even in winter. Scaling the famous Pomme d'Or (350 m), the highest ice wall in Eastern Canada, rivals even the Rockies, Alps and Pyrenees! People come from all over the world to conquer this caramel-coloured cascade of ice.

The park, with an area of 233 km², is part of the central area of the Charlevoix biosphere reserve (UNESCO). This is *drave* country (from the English word drive, as in to drive logs), and it is from this region that Félix-Antoine Savard was inspired for his novel *Menaud, maître-draveur* (1937). In fact the visitor centre (centre d'acceuil) is located in the old guard house of the Érables lock built in 1958 to float the logs.

Guided visits are organized. Mountain bikes and canoes can be rented from the visitor centre (centre d'acceuil). Cruises in river boats (*bateau-mouche*) along the Rivière Malbaie are also offered, these last 1h30 (☎ 418-665-7527).

Access: the park is located 45 km north of La Malbaie. Route 138 to Saint-Aimé-des-Lacs, then follow the signs for the park. Be sure to fill your gas tank ahead of time, because there are no service stations near the park.
☎ (418) 439-4402

Mont des Érables

Level of Difficulty: ⌂⌂⌂
Total Distance: *8.8 km return*
Change in Altitude: *780 m*
Starting Point: *parking lot near the Pont des Érables (bridge).*

The name of this trail translates literally as "maple mountain". It leads through all the different types of forest in Québec, from the maple grove in the valley, through the taiga and grey pine, all the way to the alpine tundra at the summit of Mont des Érables (1,030 m). Once at the summit you will find a barren landscape covered with a carpet of moss and permafrost (ground that is frozen year-round). For a more detailed description borrow the information brochure from the visitor centre (centre d'acceuil).

The trail is very difficult and very steep. Expect therefore around six hours for a return trip. Return by the same trail from the summit of Mont des Érables.

Mont Acropole des Draveurs

Level of Difficulty: ⌂⌂⌂
Total Distance: *4.2 km return*
Change in Altitude: *790 m*
Starting Point: *Mont Acropole parking lot, close to the campsites, south of the Centre d'Acceuil (visitor centre).*

The name of this trail translates literally as "the acropolis of the log-drivers." The route follows first the Les Cascades trail. The climb then becomes quite steep and sustained. Be sure to take your time: about 2h30 to climb to the summit of Mont des Acropole des Draveurs (1,040 m), formerly known as *Cran des Écluses* (lock notch). The view from there is exceptional. The deep, narrow valley of the Rivière Malbaie and the Laurentides region unfold before your eyes! Return by the same trail.

L'Érablière

Level of Difficulty:	
Total Distance:	*1.6 km*
Change in Altitude:	*minimal*
Starting Point:	*parking lot near the Pont des Érables (bridge).*

This short trail, whose name translates literally as "the maple grove", can be hiked in less than an hour. It provides the opportunity to explore a Laurentian maple grove, containing superb giant elm trees that are over 400 years old.

Le Belvédère

Level of Difficulty:	
Total Distance:	*1.2 km return*
Change in Altitude:	*400 m*
Starting Point:	*Mont Acropole parking lot, near the campsites, south of the Centre d'Accueil (visitor centre).*

The name of this trail translates as the "lookout." This trail is not very long, but it involves some very steep climbs. Start off on the Les Cascades trail, then cut off onto Le Belvédère, which leads to a beautiful lookout point and view of the gorge of the Rivière des Martres. Return by the same trail.

Chutes du Ruisseau Blanc et du Lac Scott

Level of Difficulty:	
Total Distance:	*2.2 km return*
Change in altitude:	*minimal*
Starting Point:	*parking lot near the Équerre (the 90° bend in the river).*

The name of this trail translates literally as "white stream and Scott Lake falls." These two trails are in the northern part of the park, near the *Équerre*, the 90° bend in the river.

The Chute du Ruisseau Blanc trail is only 400 m one-way, and leads to beautiful waterfall, almost 45 m high. Return by the same trail.

The Chute du Lac Scott falls trail is 700 m one-way and also leads to a pretty waterfall. Return by the same trail. Each trail can be hiked in less than 30 minutes, both ways.

■ CEF des Palissades

Le Centre Éducatif Forestier (CEF, Forestry Education Centre) des Palissades is located 13 km north of Saint-Siméon. A mixed-forest covered massif, rocky promontories, 300 m-high escarpments and cliffs that are over 100 m high, will overwhelm hikers. The views are unforgettable.

In total there are 10 km of trail spread over three self-guided trails: the Sylvain trail (3.5 km), named after Jean Sylvain, Quebecois outdoor pioneer, leads to the Le Buton summit, which offers an exceptional view of the region; the Sabot de la Vierge (1.9 km, lady's slipper), the name of a wildflower, takes less than an hour to hike; the Aigle (4.7 km, Eagle) trail leads to the summit of the cliffs for a splendid view. An observation site provides a wide view of the Fleuve St-Laurent. Forest scavenger hunt rallies put your knowledge to the test. At press time the centre was closed. It is expected to reopen under new management soon, but be sure to call ahead first.

Access: Route 138 to Saint-Siméon.
The Route 170 for 13 km.
☎ (418) 638-2442

■ Other Hikes, Walks and Discoveries in the Charlevoix Region

- Baie-Saint-Paul; guided hikes along the Sainte-Anne sandbanks; contact Randonnées Nature-Charlevoix, ☎ (418) 435-6275

- Maritime exhibit in Saint-Joseph-de-la-Rive; old naval shipyard, visits aboard old schooners, ☎ (418) 635-1131

- Île aux Coudres; the *Tour de l'Île* (tour of the island, 26 km) can be done by foot, completely or in part, but by bike is the best way (rentals in Saint-Bernard, 34 Rue du Port, ☎ 418-438-2332); museums and windmills in Saint-Louis

- Stroll along the beach in Cap-aux-Oies

- Visit the new Musée de Charlevoix (1990), in Pointe-au-Pic, ☎ (418) 665-4411

Chaudière-Appalaches

The Chaudière-Appalaches region is made up of several small areas with very distinct geographical features. Located opposite Québec City, on the south shore of the Fleuve St-Laurent, it stretches across a vast fertile plain before slowly climbing into the foothills of the Appalachian Mountains all the way to the American border. The Rivière Chaudière, which originates in Lac Mégantic, flows through the centre of the region, then empties into the St-Laurent across from Québec City.

■ Other Hikes, Walks and Discoveries of the Chaudière-Appalaches Region

- Parc de la Chute de la Chaudière, near Charny; 35 m-high waterfall, lookout points, suspension footbridge

- Visit the Archipel de l'Isle-aux-Grues (Île aux Grues, Île aux Oies and Grosse-Île) in front of Montmagny, ☎ (418) 248-4832

- Admire the longest covered bridge in Québec (154,5 m) in Notre-Dame-des-Pins, near Saint-Georges

- Stroll along the trails of the Parc de Récréation de Frontenac, south of Thetford Mines, ☎ (418) 422-2136

Cœur-du-Québec

The Cœur-du-Québec (the heart of Québec) region is an amalgam of diverse regions located on either shore of the St-Laurent. Located halfway between Québec City and Montréal, this large region runs from north to south linking the three types of geographical formations that make up the Québec territory: the Canadian shield, the St-Laurent plain and a small parcel of the Appalachian chain. The city of Trois-Rivières is generally considered the heart of the Cœur-du-Québec region. A vast region of lakes, rivers and forests, a kingdom for hunting and fishing, opens up to the north.

■ CEF de la Plaine

The Centre Éducatif Forestier (CEF, Forestry Education Centre) de la Plaine, near Drummonville, is located in the St-Laurent plain, in the heart of a magnificent forest. During the months of September and October the centre organizes an activity with the theme "sylviculture: trade, tools and machines". It is a unique opportunity to better

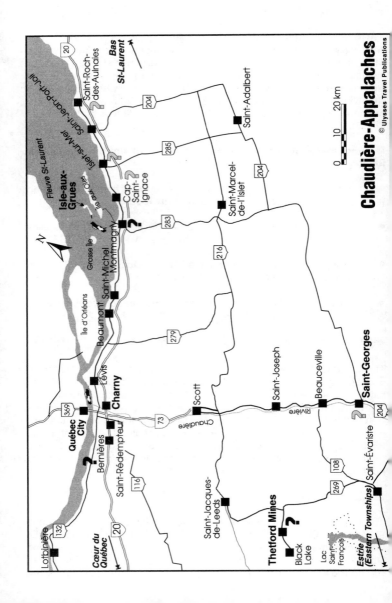

Chaudière-Appalaches

© Ulysses Travel Publications

0   10   20 km

understand professions and trades related to the cultivation and exploitation of the forest.

There are 5.7 km of trail in total, spread out over three self-guided trails and one hiking trail: the Sylvicole (1.3 km), the Ancêtres (1.25 km) and the Intermittent (1 km); and the Empreinte (2.2 km), which leads to the shores of the Rivière Saint-François. At press time the centre was closed. It is expected to reopen under new management soon, but be sure to call ahead first.

Access :   Highway 20, Exit 179, 6 km to the north on Chemin du Golf, toward Saint-Majorique.
☎ (819) 477-9533

■ **Other Hikes, Walks and Discoveries in the Cœur-du-Québec Region**

- Parc des Chutes Sainte-Ursule (waterfalls), ☎ (819) 228-3555

- Parc de la Rivière-Batiscan in Saint-Narcisse, ☎ (418) 328-3599

- Parc National de la Mauricie, ☎ (819) 536-2638; several hiking trails, including La Tourbière, Les Cascades, Lac Gabet, Triangle W.A.W., Chutes du Lac Parker and Belvédère du Lac Rosoy

- Parc des Chutes de la Petite-Rivière-Bostonnais, north of La Tuque, ☎ (819) 523-4561

- Lainerie d'Ulverton, (wool mill) near Drummonville; information centre, hiking trails, covered bridge, ☎ (819) 826-3157

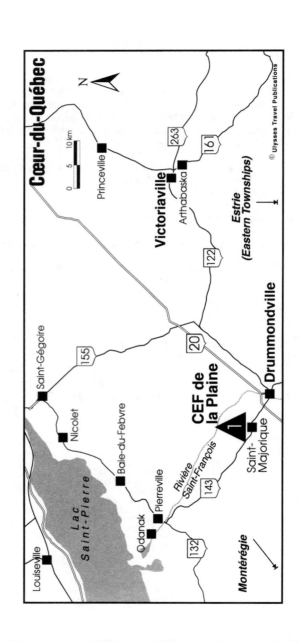

Cœur-du-Québec

N

0 5 10 km

Princeville

Victoriaville

Arthabaska

263

161

122

Estrie (Eastern Townships)

Saint-Grégoire

155

Nicolet

Baie-du-Febvre

Pierreville

Odanak

132

143

Lac Saint-Pierre

Louiseville

20

Drummondville

CEF de la Plaine

1

Saint-Majorique

Rivière Saint-François

Montérégie

© Ulysses Travel Publications

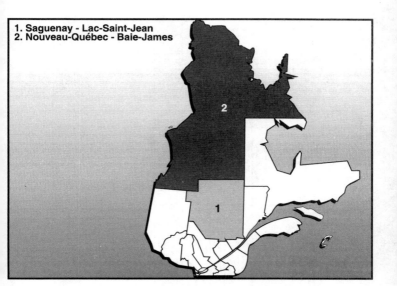

1. Saguenay - Lac-Saint-Jean
2. Nouveau-Québec - Baie-James

SAGUENAY - LAC-SAINT-JEAN AND QUÉBEC'S FAR NORTH

The southermost fjord in the world, the Rivière Saguenay originates in Lac Saint-Jean, a veritable inland sea with a diameter of over 35 km. These two impressive bodies of water form the backbone of the magnificent Saguenay — Lac-Saint-Jean tourist region.

This chapter also offers a glimpse at the hiking opportunities of Québec's far north, in the Nouveau-Québec — Baie-James tourist region.

Saguenay - Lac-Saint-Jean

Moving swiftly toward the Fleuve St-Laurent, the Rivière Saguenay flows through a rugged landscape studded with cliffs and mountains.

SAGUENAY - LAC-SAINT-JEAN AND QUÉBEC'S FAR NORTH

	Level of Difficulty of Hike	Total Distance of Hike (km)	Change in Altitude (m)	Page
SHORT HIKES				
Parc du Saguenay : de méandres à falaises	◁	1.6	50	118
Parc du Saguenay : La Statue	◁	7.0	260	118
Parc du Saguenay : Des Chutes	◁◁◁	13.0	550	120
Parc du Saguenay : Le Fjord	◁◁◁	12.0	300	121
Parc du Saguenay : De la Coupe and De la Pointe-de-l'Islet	◁	2.0	faible	121
LONG HIKES				
Parc du Saguenay : Les Caps	◁◁◁	25.0	350	120

The Saguenay is navigable as far as Chicoutimi, and governed by the eternal rhythm of the tides. In the summer, its rich marine animal life includes various species of whales. Further north, Lac Saint-Jean's brilliant and abundant waters feed the Rivière Saguenay. The sweet and delicious blueberries that abound in the area have made the region of Lac Saint-Jean famous. In fact, the fruit is so closely linked with the region, that Quebecois across the province have adopted the term *bleuets* (blueberries) as an affectionate nickname for the local inhabitants.

■ Parc du Saguenay

Parc du Saguenay has plenty to offer hikers. The trail network here is definitely one of the fastest-growing in Québec. Each season, a new trail, or new section of trail is cleared. And along with the hiking trails, horseback-riding trails are also being laid-out.

Today there are over 100 km of hiking trails in the park. Walking or hiking, for one day or longer — the choice is as extensive as the terrain and environment are varied (beaches, sand dunes, cliffs, rocky capes, etc.).

Covering 284 km², Parc du Saguenay was created in 1983 to preserve the shores of this magnificent, deep, 100 km-long fjord. A veritable arctic maritime enclave in Québec, the Saguenay fjord is one of the 20 longest in the world!

As well as the 750 celebrated belugas (small white whales) that live here, there are whales, dolphins, porpoises and seals. Most of the whale-watching cruises in the area leave from Tadoussac. And a visit to the region without some sort of "intimate" encounter with these creatures is almost unimaginable.

The governments of Québec and Canada have undertaken to manage the Parc Marin du Saguenay, in order to protect the natural phenomena of the area.

A visit to the Centre d'Interprétation de Baie-Éternité and to the Maison des Dunes (information centres) will sensitize any visitor to the beauty and fragility of such an environment. If you would like to know even more about the marine mammals, visits to the information centres in Baie-Sainte-Catherine, Tadoussac and Cap-de-Bon-Désir are a must.

Access: south shore; Route 138, then Route 170, which passes by Petit-Saguenay, Anse Saint-Jean and Rivière-Éternité.

north shore; Route 138 to Baie-Sainte-Catherine, then take the ferry to Tadoussac. Route 172 follows the Rivière Saguenay all the way to Chicoutimi.

Parc du Saguenay ☎ (418) 544-7388
Accueil Rivière-Éternité ☎ (418) 272-4238
Accueil Tadoussac ☎ (418) 235-4238

De Méandres à Falaises

Level of Difficulty:
Total Distance: *1.6 km loop*
Change in Altitude: *50 m*
Starting Point: *Centre d'Interprétation (information centre) in Baie-Éternité.*

The name of this trail translates literally as "meanderings at the cliffs." This is a small self-guided nature trail, with information panels along the way that explain the various natural phenomena of the bay. The trail also leads to the foot of the cliffs of Cap Trinité, a majestic cape measuring 350 m.

La Statue

Level of Difficulty:
Total Distance: *7 km return*
Change in Altitude: *260 m*
Starting Point: *Centre d'Interprétation (information centre) in Baie-Éternité.*

This trail is not very difficult, but it is not very easy either. It is well laid-out and marked, and the stairways and platforms help hikers negociate the steeper more difficult sections.

The trail climbs from the start. Beautiful views of Baie Éternité are possible along the way. A shelter at the summit of Cap Éternité is open for hikers to take a break and have a snack. The trail then leads to the 9 m-high statue of the virgin, called Notre-Dame de Saguenay (Our Lady of the Saguenay). The view of the fjord from the statue is very impressive. Return by the same trail.

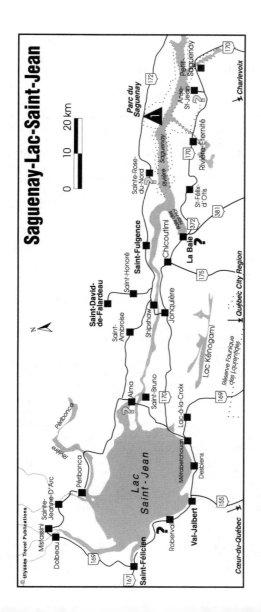

Saguenay-Lac-Saint-Jean

Les Caps

Level of Difficulty:	⛰ *(3 days)* or ⛰⛰ *(2 days)*
Total Distance:	*25 km (one way only)*
Change in Altitude:	*350 m*
Starting Point:	*Centre d'Interprétation (information centre) in Baie-Éternité.*

The Les Caps long hiking trail (with overnights) is one of the most spectacular in Québec. It links the Baie de la Rivière Éternité and the town of L'Anse Saint-Jean (*anse* means cove). A walk along the plateau follows the cape and cliffs as well as the fjord of the Saguenay. Since this is a linear trail, you will need another car at the other end. Reservations for camping or staying in the shelters is also required (Société de Développement Touristique de Rivière-Éternité ☎ 418-272-3008).

There are two ways to complete the Les Caps trails. The first, and easier way, takes three days and two nights in comfortable shelters; it involves less than four hours of walking per day. The second option is more difficult and takes two days, with an overnight in a tent on the shores of Lac de la Goutte. Expect six hours of walking per day, and don't forget that you will be carrying a heavy bag with lots of gear. The beautiful scenery makes up for the extra little bit of exertion though!

Take your time admiring the majestic Cap Trinité. An impressive three hundred and fifity metres of compacted rock tower ominously over the Rivière Saguenay. You may even see the rock-climbers at work. The walls of Cap Trinité are the highest rock-climbing faces in the province of Québec. The trail leads to the town of L'Anse Saint-Jean.

Take note that the Les Caps trail does continue for another 10 km to the pier of the Petit-Saguenay. This section can be hiked seperately.

Des Chutes

Level of Difficulty:	⛰⛰
Total Distance:	*13 km return*
Change in Altitude:	*550 m*
Starting Point:	*Rang St-Thomas Nord in L'Anse Saint-Jean.*

This trail leads to the summit of the second highest summit in the region, Montagne Blanche (White Mountain). It passes close to two magnificent waterfalls (*chutes*), one of which is close to 100 m high.

The town and cove of L'Anse Saint-Jean and the fjord of the Saguenay are both visible from the trail. At the intersection, head south to climb to the summit of Montagne Blanche (570 m), from where the view of the fjord and the mountains is paticulalrly beautiful. Return by the same trail.

Le Fjord

Level of Difficulty:	◪ ◪
Total Distance:	*12 km (return)*
Change in Altitude:	*300 m*
Starting Point:	*Cap de la Boule or the Accueil (visitor centre) of the park in Tadoussac.*

The Le Fjord trail is considered one of the most beautiful in Québec. Inaugurated just two years ago, this linear trail was just crying out to be created. Breathtaking views are found at every turn along the trail: the widest part of the fjord, the bays, capes, cliff walls and the town of Tadoussac at the mouth of the Saguenay. A trail as visually stunning as this is rare.

The Le Fjord trail is 12 km long and takes four hours to hike, the usual route being to start at Cap de la Boule and end up at the visitor centre of the park in Tadoussac (there is a bus from here to Cap de la Boule; for information ☎ 418-235-4238). This route avoids the 300 m-long haul from Tadoussac up to the plateau.

De la Coupe and De la Pointe-de-l'Islet

Level of Difficulty:	◪
Total Distance:	*2 km loop*
Change of Altitude:	*minimal*
Starting Point:	*Accueil (visitor centre) of the park in Tadoussac.*

These two small self-guided nature trails, which make two short loops, provide an overview of the region and of the fjord of the Saguenay. The De la Coupe trail leads to the summits of the small mountains in Anse à l'Eau cove, while the De la Pointe-de-l'Islet trail is a good point from which to watch the marine mammals at the mouth of the Saguenay.

Variation: It is also possible to hike along the beach from the Baie de Tadoussac to the Baie du Moulin in Baude. This 6 km-long trail (one way) leads to the Maison des Dunes (information centre).

■ **Other Hikes, Walks and Discoveries in the Saguenay — Lac-Saint-Jean Region**

- The historic village of Val-Jalbert, near Chambord; ghost town, Chute Ouiatchouan (waterfall), chairlift, hiking trails, ☎ (418) 275-3132

- Jardin Zoologique de Saint-Félicien, a terrific zoo where the roles are reversed and you are the caged animal! ☎ 1-800-667-5687 or (418) 679-0543

- Parc de la Pointe-Taillon, on the shores of Lac Saint-Jean; hiking, beach, water sports, ☎ (418) 695-2644

- Centre Plein Air Bec-Scie, outdoor centre in La Baie; 25 km of hiking trails, ☎ (418) 544-5433

- Centre d'Interprétation des Battures et de Réhabilitation des Oiseaux, Wetlands and Bird Rehabilitation Information Centre, in Saint-Fulgence, ☎ (418) 674-2425

- Parc Régional des Monts-Valin, near Saint-David-de-Falardeau; hiking and wildlife observation, ☎ 1-800-463-9651

Nouveau-Québec - Baie-James

The geographic area encompassing the tourist regions of Nouveau-Québec and Baie-James is a gigantic northern territory, stretching from the 49th parallel north to the 62nd parallel and covering more than half of the area of Québec. The rough beauty of this barren landscape, its harsh winter climate and its unique tundra vegetation giving way to taiga and then Boreal forest, create a region completely different from the rest of Québec. Though some travellers do venture northward, this vast territory really remains the land of the northern Native peoples. The Inuit live in small communities in the far north along Hudson Bay, Hudson Strait and Ungava Bay, while the Cree Indians live mostly in the taiga and along the shores of James Bay.

Northern Québec is not lacking in attractions. The vast wilderness and rich flora and fauna are attracting more and more nature lovers.

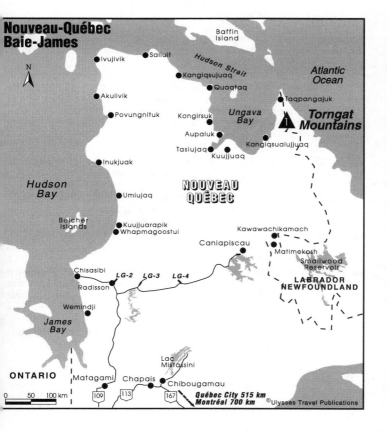

■ **Torngat Mountains**

The Torngat Mountains, located in the northeastern extremity of Québec, straddling the border of Labrador, between Ungava Bay and the Labrador Sea, represents the highest chain of mountains in Québec. These lunar landscapes leave lasting impressions on the minds of all hikers who explore them.

In the Torngat ("mountains of the evil spirits" in Inuktitut) Mountains the aurora borealis, also known as the northern lights come to wish you goodnight!

There is no road in to the mountains. To get there you will have to fly to Kuujjuaq and from there take a bush plane into the heart of the mountains, where there is no landing strip — not the time to realize you have left your sleeping bag at home!

Two hundred twenty kilometres long and one hundred kilometres wide, the Torngat Mountains cover as much area as the Alps, with altitudes of close to 1,600 m. Several of the summits are close to 1,700 m.

Summer lasts about 2 months, with 18 hours of sunshine per day. During this northern summer, the tundra is transformed into an expanse of beautiful little flowers. Visitors can expect to see caribous, black bears, wolves and eagles.

The hikes lead across mountains, fjords and glaciers. Though the hikes are generally not very difficult, anyone planning to organize their own expedition should only do so if they have extensive experience and knowledge of hiking and outdoor adventuring (maps, compass, first aid, security, etc.).

For those looking for a guide, contact **Passe Montagne**, ☎ 1-800-465-2123 or (819) 322-2123.

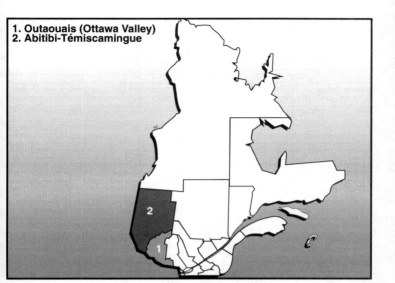

1. Outaouais (Ottawa Valley)
2. Abitibi-Témiscamingue

WESTERN QUÉBEC

The Outaouais (Ottawa Valley) and Abitibi regions are the westernmost regions of Québec. Although discovered early on by explorers and trappers, the Outaouais region was not colonized until the beginning of the 19th century thanks to the initiatives of Loyalists arriving from the United States. Forestry, in particular the exploitation of white and red pine, ideal for maritime construction, was for a long time the principle economic activity of the region.

As for Abitibi-Témiscamingue, it was not until the beginning of the 20th century that colonization started, with the glorious days of the gold rush.

Outaouais

A region of rolling hills, lakes and waterways, including the magnificent Parc de la Gatineau, opens up directly north of the cities of Hull,

WESTERN QUÉBEC

	Level of Difficulty of Hike	Total Distance of Hike (km)	Change in Altitude (m)	Page
SHORT HIKES				
Parc de la Gatineau: Larriault	⊿	3.0	60	128
Parc de la Gatineau: Mont King	⊿	2.5	70	129
Parc de la Gatineau: Champlain	⊿	1.2	20	129
Parc de la Gatineau: Lac Pink	⊿	1.4	20	130
Parc de la Gatineau: Caverne Lusk	⊿	10.0	100	130
Parc d'Aiguebelle: La Traverse	⊿	3.0	50	133
Parc d'Aiguebelle: L'Escalade	⊿	2.6	160	133
Parc d'Aiguebelle: Les Marmites	⊿	1.8	70	134
Parc d'Aiguebelle: L'Aventurier	⊿⊿	10.0	50	134
Parc d'Aiguebelle: Les Versants	⊿⊿	11.0	40	134
Parc d'Aiguebelle: Mont Dominant	⊿⊿	8.0	200	135

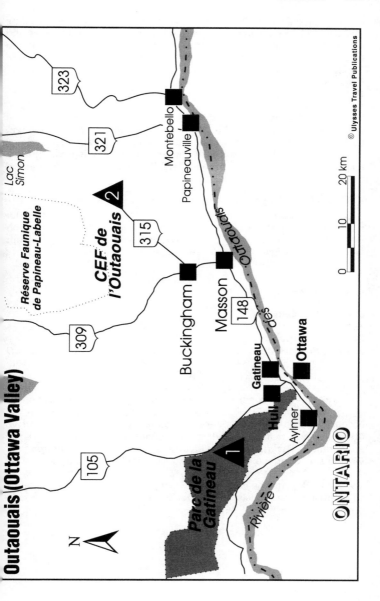

Outaouais (Ottawa Valley)

CEF de l'Outaouais 2

Parc de la Gatineau 1

Réserve Faunique de Papineau-Labelle

Lac Simon

Montebello

Papineauville

Buckingham

Masson

Gatineau

Hull

Aylmer

Ottawa

ONTARIO

Rivière des Outaouais

323
321
315
309
105
148

N

0   10   20 km

© Ulysses Travel Publications

Gatineau and Aylmer. The park is the location of the Canadian Prime Minister's official summer residence and a beautiful spot for hikes and walks. The city of Hull, which faces Ottawa across the river, is home to one of the most interesting museums in the country: the Musée Canadien des Civilisations.

■ Parc de la Gatineau

Parc de la Gatineau, located northwest of the city of Hull in the Outaouais region, is relatively unknown by most hikers in Québec. Located just minutes from Hull and Ottawa, this park has close to 200 km of hiking trails to explore! The hikes are diversified, informative and accessible to all. The National Trail (Sentier National) has passed through the park since 1992.

Access: from the city of Hull, take Highway 5 north, Exit 12 (Old Chelsea). Turn left onto Chemin Old Chelsea and follow it for 3 km (Centre d'Accueil Old Chelsea Information Centre). This is the park entrance for all hikes except "Caverne Lusk" (see below).
☎ (819) 827-2020

Larriault

Level of Difficulty:
Total Distance: *3 km loop*
Change in Altitude: *60 m*
Starting Point: *Belvédère Larriault (lookout point) parking lot, in front of the Lac Mulvihill parking lot.*

This trail crosses a superb beech and maple forest. Near the beginning of the trail there is a climb up to a lookout point that is worth the detour. Retrace your steps back to the main trail, which leads to two other lookout points, including one over the falls (superb in the springtime). The trail then follows a stream up to the Promenade Champlain. Continue toward Lac Mulvihill and the parking lot.

Variation: Beyond the Promenade Champlain, a trail on the right leads to Moorside, the mansion of former Canadian Prime Minister, Mackenzie-King (☎ 819-827-3405).

Mont King

Level of Difficulty:	
Total Distance:	*2.5 km loop*
Change in Altitude:	*70 m*
Starting Point:	*Lac Black parking lot.*

This small self-guided nature trail includes 10 observation points. Mont King is part of the Eardley Escarpment, a 30 km-long rock wall that rises above the Outaouais valley.

The trail begins by climbing the north side of Mont King up to the summit where white and red oak cohabit (unique to Québec). From there the view of the Rivière Outaouais, Lac des Montagnes and the escarpment is exceptional. It is common, particularly in the spring, to see birds of prey swooping on the rising currents of air in the valley. The trail then heads down to the parking lot.

Champlain

Level of Difficulty:	
Total Distance:	*1.2 km loop*
Change in Altitude:	*15 m*
Starting Point:	*Belvédère Champlain (lookout point).*

The Champlain trail follows the Eardley Escarpment. This self-guided nature trail includes eight observation points.

After crossing a ravine typical of the Canadian Shield, hikers will come upon a microclimate (an area where the climate is different from the surroundings, hot and dry in this case) conducive to the growth of rare plants. The trail passes near an erratic block, left behind after the thawing of a glacier, then returns to the starting point.

Lac Pink

Level of Difficulty:	
Total Distance:	*1.4 km*
Change in Altitude:	*20 m*
Starting Point:	*Lac Pink parking lot.*

This trail follows the shores of Lac Pink. Research in this lake lead to the discovery of a salt water fish that had adapted to fresh water, as well as a prehistoric bacteria.

The trail has been carefully laid out to protect the shores of Lac Pink, the very existence of which is threatened. Panels along the trail provide a better understanding of the life of this lake.

Caverne Lusk

Level of Difficulty:	
Total Distance:	*10 km return*
Change in Altitude:	*100 m*
Starting Point:	*parking lot at Plage Parent (beach), on Lac Philippe. To get there take Route 105 Nord, then Route 366 Ouest toward Sainte-Cécile-de-Masham turn left at the sign for Lac Philippe.*

This trail leads to a real cave that hikers can explore (the cave has two parts). It is an ideal to spot to see if you like for speleology!

From the Parent Beach (*plage*), the trail follows Lac Philippe to the Smith Beach, then joins trail # 50 to the end of the lake where it branches off onto trail # 54, and then up to an intersection. Turn right here and 500 m after passing a beaver dam, Caverne Lusk appears. Two information panels provide information on the grotto. Return by the same trail.

Variation: It is possible to do a loop by passing Lac Lusk and a large field. This loop is 14 km in total.

■ CEF de l'Outaouais

The Centre Éducatif Forestier (CEF, Forestry Education Centre) de l'Outaouais is located northeast of Buckingham. The centre is also called "big tree country." Red oak and white pine dominate the area from their tree tops some 30 m above the ground!

White-tailed deer, slow-moving turtles and woodpeckers frequent the forests of the centre.

There are 7.2 km of trails to cover, spread out over five self-guided nature trails: the Cendré trail (2.1 km loop) leads to a fantastic view of Lac la Blanche; the Prucheraie trail (900 m return) crosses a 250 year-old hemlock spruce (*pruche*) forest; the Ouaouaron trail (2,4 km loop) is an aquatic trail (with long footbridges) along Lac Amik (beaver in Algonquian) and Lac aux Hérons; the Forestier trail (1.3 km loop) crosses first a young, and then a mature, forest before reaching a pretty lookout point over Lac Amik.

Booklets and games, including a labyrinth, will keep the young, and not so young, busy. At press time the centre was closed. It is expected to reopen under new management soon, but be sure to call ahead first.

Access: from Buckingham, take Route 315 toward Lac la Blanche (18 km).
☎ (819) 986-2183

■ Other Hikes, Walks and Discoveries in the Outaouais Region

● North Nation Mills (Chutes de Plaisance); waterfalls, lookout points, hiking, ☎ (819) 427-5363

● Réserve Faunique de Papineau-Labelle; trails to Mont Devlin and Mont Bondy, ☎ (819) 454-2013

● Réserve Faunique de Plaisance; the Zizanie-des-Marais trail as well as the Randonnée des Baladeurs trail, ☎ (819) 427-5334

● Réserve Faunique de La Vérendrye; several self-guided nature trails, including the Chutes du Lac Roland trail, the Forêt-Mystérieuse trail at Lac de la Vieille as well as the Pointe au Lac Jean-Péré trail, ☎ (819) 438-2017

Abitibi-Témiscamingue

Along with Québec's far north and James Bay, the region of Abitibi-Témiscamingue is one of the final frontiers of Québec. Though the fertile territory bordering Lac Témiscamingue was inhabited as of the last century, colonization for the most part only began at the beginning of the 20th century. The region is crossed by an invisible line which divides the drainage of the land; to one side rainfall flows north toward James Bay, while on the other side it flows toward the Fleuve

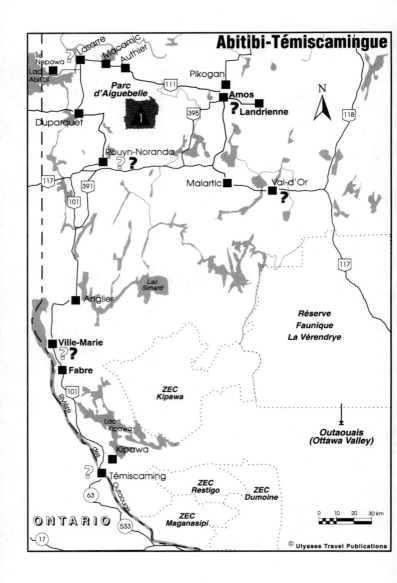

Abitibi-Témiscamingue

Lasarre
Île Nepawa
Lac Abitibi
Macamic
Authier
Pikogan
111
Parc d'Aiguebelle
Amos
395
Landrienne
118
N
Duparquet
Rouyn-Noranda
117
391
101
Malartic
Val-d'Or
117
Lac Simard
Anglier
Réserve Faunique La Vérendrye
Ville-Marie
Fabre
101
ZEC Kipawa
Outaouais (Ottawa Valley)
Rivière
Lac Kipawa
Kipawa
des
Témiscaming
ZEC Restigo
ZEC Dumoine
63
Outaouais
ONTARIO
533
ZEC Maganasipi
0 10 20 30 km
17
© Ulysses Travel Publications

St-Laurent. The terrain of the region is, however, quite flat. Hikers come to relive the adventure of a real gold rush, but mostly to take in the vast expanse of territory, the huge forests and the countless lakes.

■ Parc d'Aiguebelle

Parc d'Aiguebelle is definitely one of Québec's best-kept secrets. Very few hikers actually know it exists, yet its 30 km of trails would marvel even the most seasoned among them.

There are no huge mountains here (Mont Dominant, at 566 m is the highest point in all of Abitibi), but more than thirty interesting geological and geomorphologic phenomena can be observed.The rock formations in the park are the result of volcanic activity some 2.7 billion years ago!

Access: Parc d'Aiguebelle is located between the cities of Val-d'Or, Amos, LaSarre and Rouyn-Noranda. It is 110 km from Val-d'Or, passing by Mont-Brun, to the entrance of the park (Mont-Brun sector).
☎ (819) 637-7322

La Traverse

Level of Difficulty:
Total Distance: *3 km loop*
Change in Altitude: *50 m*
Starting Point: *Lac La Haie sector parking lot.*

This is a superb little hike with several beautiful lookout points along the way. The suspension footbridge over Lac La Haie makes for a particularly impressive crossing!

L'Escalade

Level of Difficulty:
Total Distance: *2.6 km return*
Change in Altitude: *160 m*
Starting Point: *Lac La Haie sector parking lot.*

This short trail is actually relatively steep. Begin by following the La Traverse trail for 360 m, then follow L'Escalade directly up to the summit of La Trompeuse and the La Cigale shelter where a beautiful view awaits. Return by the same trail.

Les Marmites

Level of Difficulty:	⌂
Total Distance:	*1.8 km loop*
Change in Altitude:	*70 m*
Starting Point:	*Lac La Haie sector parking lot.*

The accent of this short self-guided nature trail is on the history of the Abitibi and Parc d'Aiguebelle countryside.

L'Aventurier

Level of Difficulty:	⌂ ⌂
Total Distance:	*10 km loop*
Change in Altitude:	*50 m*
Starting Point:	*Lac La Haie sector parking lot.*

This trail is more difficult because it not as well laid-out as the other trails in the park. It does however loop around magnificent Lac La Haie. At the beginning, follow the La Traverse trail to the suspension footbridge (1.5 km) at which point you should follow the L'Aventurier trail.

Les Versants

Level of Difficulty:	⌂ ⌂
Total Distance:	*11 km return*
Change in Altitude:	*40 m*
Starting Point:	*Lac Sault sector parking lot.*

Begin by following the Les Paysages trail for 1.2 km. There are some beautiful lookout points, in particular, the Belvédère Le Corbeau. The trail passes near Lac de la Muraille before running alongside Lac Sault up to Lac Perché. The most beautiful waterfall in the park can seen here in the spring. The trail ends at the intersection with the Le Partage trail. Return by the same trail.

Variation: If your group has two cars at its disposal (if not, ask around to see if there are any hikers who want to share the experience), it is possible to explore Lac La Haie and Lac Sault in one day. To do so, leave one car at the Lac Sault sector parking lot and the other at the Lac La Haie lot, from where the hike will start.

Start off on the Les Marmites trail to the suspension footbridge, then follow the L'Aventurier trail to the end of Lac La Haie, where you will take the Le Partage trail to the Les Versants trail around Lac Sault. At the end of Lac Sault follow the Les Paysages trail to end up at the Lac Sault sector parking lot.

The Le Partage trail is so called because it follows the line that divides the drainage for the waters of the area (*partage* means division). Therefore, Lac La Haie flows south toward the Fleuve St-Laurent, while Lac Sault flows north toward James Bay!

The linear hike is 11 km from one parking lot to the other.

Mont Dominant

Level of Difficulty:	🗻🗻
Total Distance:	*8 km return*
Change in Altitude:	*200 m*
Starting Point:	*Mont Dominant sector parking lot.*

This trail leads to the summit of Mont Dominant, which, at 566 m, is the highest summit in the Abitibi region. The view from the summit of Mont Dominant is, shall we say ... very "dominating!" Unfortunately the communication towers detract from the natural beauty of this space. Return by the same trail.

■ **Other Hikes, Walks and Discoveries in the Abitibi-Témiscamingue Region**

- Centre des Marais et ses Habitants (marshlands habitat centre), in Amos; rehabilitation of injured animals, ☎ (819) 732-6875

- Musée de la Faune (wildlife museum), in Landrienne; 300 stuffed wild animals, ☎ (819) 732-4387

- Lieu Historique National de Fort-Témiscamingue National Historic Site, in Ville-Marie; ruins of an old fur-trading post, famous "enchanted forest" with oddly shaped thuyas (a type of coniferous tree), ☎ (819) 629-3222

- The Rivière Kipawa, 10 km south of the town of Fabre; beautiful 6.4 km-long hiking trail (waterfalls, rapids, potholes)

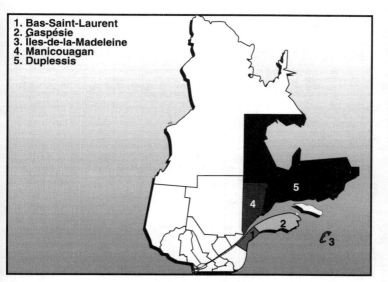

1. Bas-Saint-Laurent
2. Gaspésie
3. Îles-de-la-Madeleine
4. Manicouagan
5. Duplessis

EASTERN QUÉBEC

The picturesque region of Bas-Saint-Laurent extends east along the Fleuve St-Laurent from the little town of La Pocatière to the village of Sainte-Luce, and south to the borders of the United States and New Brunswick.

The shores of the vast Gaspé peninsula are washed by the waters of Baie des Chaleurs, the St-Laurent and its gulf. This is a cherished vacation spot for many Quebecois.

The Îles-de-la-Madeleine islands form one of the most breathtaking regions in Québec! An atmosphere that is distinctly Quebecois pervades, yet you may also feel like you are in Acadia, Normandy or even the Caribbean; and you will wish you never had to leave!

The Manicouagan region stretches for 300 km along the north shore of the St-Laurent and northward into the Laurentian plateau to include the Groulx Mountains and the Manicouagan Reservoir.

EASTERN QUÉBEC

	Level of Difficulty of Hike	Total Distance of Hike (km)	Change in Altitude (m)	Page
SHORT HIKES				
Parc du Bic: Tour of Cap à l'Orignal (along the trails)	◁◁	7.0	95	142
Parc du Bic: La Pinède	◁◁	5.8	140	142
Parc du Bic: Tour of Cap à l'Orignal (along the coast)	◁◁	9.0	95	143
Parc du Bic: Pic Champlain	◁	4.4	245	143
Parc du Bic: Îlet au Flacon	◁	1.0	minimal	143
Parc de la Gaspésie: Mont Jacques-Cartier	◁◁	8.2	477	147
Parc de la Gaspésie: Mont Albert	◁◁◁	13.0	885	148
Parc de la Gaspésie: Mont Richardson	◁◁	11.6	610	148
Parc de la Gaspésie: Lac aux Américains	◁	2.6	90	149
Parc de la Gaspésie: Pic du Brûlé	◁◁	13.2	368	149
Parc Forillon: A Tour of the Area	◁	3.0	75	150
Parc Forillon: Les Graves	◁	13.2	90	151
Parc Forillon: Mont Saint-Alban	◁	8.5	250	151
Parc de l'Île-Bonaventure-et-du-Rocher-Percé: Tour of the Island	◁	8.4	120	152
Île Grande Basque: Tour of Île Grande Basque	◁	9.0	100	158
LONG HIKES				
Parc de la Gaspésie: McGerrigle Trail	◁◁	23.0	1 070	149

Finally, the Duplessis region covers a vast remote region bound by the gulf of the St-Laurent for almost a thousand kilometres and by the Labrador border. Its small population of francophones, anglophones and Montagnais, is spread out mainly along the coast of the gulf, and in a few inland mining towns.

These five regions make up the area of "Eastern Québec" covered in this chapter.

Bas-Saint-Laurent

In addition to the particularly fertile areas next to the river, much of the Bas-Saint-Laurent region consists of forestry land, and gently rolling hills glittering with lakes and streams.

■ Islands of the Bas-Saint-Laurent

The islands of the Bas-Saint-Laurent region are located in the Fleuve St-Laurent at the city of Rivière-du-Loup. The Société Duvetnor, a private non-profit organization devoted to the conservation of the wildlife and habitat in the estuary of the St-Laurent, began purchasing these islands in 1984, to preserve the habitat of several aquatic birds that live here (eider ducks, great herons, small penguins, egret cormorants, etc.).

The islands of the Bas-Saint-Laurent are made up of the **Îles du Pot à l'Eau-de-Vie** (brandy bottle island), **Île aux Lièvres** (hare island) and the **Archipel Les Pèlerins** (pilgrim archipelago). Hiking and walking on the islands has been possible since 1989, when the Société Duvetnor bought a boat and developed a network of hiking trails.

Grey seals lounging on the beach, cliffs dotted with thousands of little penguins, deserted stretches of sand, eider ducks, historic lighthouses, peaceful coves, wide open views and much more fill the senses of hikers in the area.

Several discovery and guided-cruise packages are offered. From simple hour and a half-long cruises to extended hikes with overnights in tents on Île aux Lièvres, hikers will have no problem planning the perfect itinerary.

Do not forget to reserve well in advance, since space on the boat is limited and departure dates vary depending on the tides.

Access: by boat, from the ferry pier in Rivière-du-Loup. Société Duvetnor ☎ (418) 867-1660

Îles du Pot à l'Eau-de-Vie

The Gros Pot (big jar) and the Pot du Phare (lighthouse jar) form the islands known as the Îles du Pot à l'Eau-de-Vie. Several trails cross these islands, some of which were laid out by the first inhabitants of the archipelago. The La Chaloupe, La Petite Traverse, L'Anse du Sud-Ouest and L'Épitaphe trails cover the island called Pot du Phare. The last one, L'Épitaphe, leads to the epitaph of a soldier who died on the island in 1814.

The Pot du Phare island houses a magnificent historic lighthouse (*phare*) which offers an expansive view of the immense estuary. Accommodation is available in one of the three rooms in the lighthouse, allowing hikers to take full advantage of a visit to the island. The *Nuitée au Phare* (lighthouse overnight) is a lodging package which includes a guided excursion and three delicious meals (fine regional cuisine). Wake up to the cries of seagulls, the coos of eider ducks and the morning mist!

Île aux Lièvres

Île aux Lièvres, 13 km long and more than 1.5 km wide, has a 40 km-long network of hiking trails. Île aux Lièvres is the largest inhabited (by humans) island in the whole St-Laurent.

The hardest part about the island is choosing how to explore it, because you will want to see it all. The guide on staff can help you choose between the many trails, like the La Crête, Le Jardin, Eiders, La Mer and the Grande Course trails. In the centre of the island an 86 m-high ridge offers a grand view of the estuary. Sandy beaches on the north shore of the island are an ideal spot to relax. A small garden with wild parsley and sea rye growing side by side is located on the point of the island. The south shore is pocketed by pretty little coves where eider ducks can be seen.

Camping is now possible on the island, giving visitors the chance to watch the night fall and enjoy the celestial beauty of the night sky!

■ Parc du Bic

Parc du Bic is located between the towns of Bic and Saint-Fabien, and was created in 1984 to protect a part of the estuary's coastline.

With an area of 33 km², this park juts into the river and is made up of several islands and peninsulas. Capes and rocky points, as well as bays and coves, form the magnificent countryside of Parc du Bic.

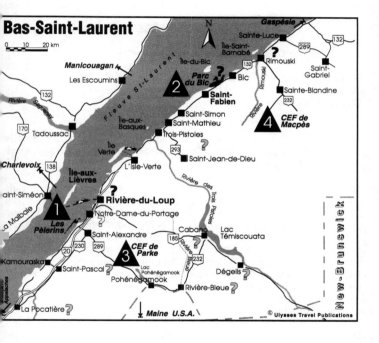

The cold, salty waters of the Fleuve St-Laurent are home to a diverse flora and fauna. Seagulls, cormorants and eider ducks rub shoulders with grey and common seals. It is even possible to harvest mussels and clams.

Ten kilometres of hiking trails help visitors discover the marvels of this park. There are also several kilometres to be covered along the coast, at low tide.

Access: Route 132. After the town of Saint-Fabien, use the Cap-à-l'Orignal entrance.
               ☎ (418) 869-3502, 736-5035

Tour of Cap à l'Orignal (along the trails)

Level of Difficulty:
Total Distance: *7 km loop*
Change in Altitude: *95 m*
Starting Point: *the Rioux farm parking lot.*

The hike does the tour of Cap à l'Orignal (moose cape) as well as the Montagne à Michaud along the Contrebandier, Miquelon, Escaliers and Scoggan trails.

The Contrebandier trail which leads to the cove Anse à Mouille-Cul, was used by dealers of contraband to get illegal alcohol during the prohibition years. The route then follows the Miquelon trail, named after the whisky from the French islands of Saint-Pierre and Miquelon, before branching off onto the Escaliers trail up to the summit of Montagne à Michaud and then joining the Scoggan trail. This last trail, named after the Canadian botanist Homer J. Scoggan, heads down and east to the cove Anse à Damase, from where you can retrace your steps to the parking lot.

La Pinède

Level of Difficulty:
Total Distance: *5.8 km return*
Change in Altitude: *140 m*
Starting Point: *Rioux farm parking lot.*

The name of this trail translates literally as "the pine grove." To begin follow the Scoggan trail which climbs to the west, for over 100 m to the intersection of the La Pinède trail. This trail is 1 km long and climbs to an altitude of 140 m on the southern side of Montagne à Michaud. The view of Baie des Ha! Ha!, Île du Bic and the cove Anse à l'Orignal is truly superb. The trail allows hikers to observe the magnificent hundred-year-old grey pines. Return by the same trail.

Tour of Cap à l'Orignal (along the coast)

Level of Difficulty:
Total Distance: *9 km loop*
Change in Altitude: *95 m*
Starting Point: *Rioux farm parking lot.*

This trail is not marked. As well, hikers must check the tide schedule at the information centre (Centre d'Interprétation) before venturing forth. The trail follows the coast (where the sea meets the land), from the coves Anse à Wilson to Anse à Damase, then along Anse à Voilier (sailboat cove), before running along Cap à l'Orignal to end up in Anse à Mouille-Cul (wet bum cove)! From there, continue west along the cliffs of Montagne à Michaud to the fork at Louison, where you will follow the Scoggan trail from west to east to Anse à Damase. The tour requires about three hours of walking.

Pic Champlain

Level of Difficulty:
Total Distance: *4.4 km return*
Change in Altitude: *245 m*
Starting Point: *Pic Champlain parking lot.*

The Pic Champlain trail is not very difficult or very long. Just a few huffs and puffs and you are at the top. From the summit at 345 m, the view of the bay is particularly spectacular. A lookout point provides a better perspective of the panorama. Return by the same trail.

Îlet au Flacon

Level of Difficulty:
Total Distance: *1 km*
Change in Altitude: *minimal*
Starting Point: *Îlet au Flacon parking lot near Saint-Fabien-sur-Mer.*

This magnificent little loop trail takes only about thirty minutes to hike, passing by the coves Anse à Mercier and Anse à Capelans. The trail is located in the western part of the park and is not marked.

■ CEF de Parke

The Centre Éducatif Forestier (CEF, Forestry Education Centre) de Parke, located southwest of the city of Rivière-du-Loup, is surrounded by wooded hills, rivers and three lakes.

There are 11 km of trail: four self-guided nature trails and one hike. The Le Lacustre trail (1.3 km loop) goes around Lac Parke; the Le Forestier trail (2.4 km loop) leads to a forest of pine and spruce, where traces of a forest fire can be seen; the Le Labyrinthe trail (500 m loop) includes a little game; the Le Marais trail (2.2 km loop) goes around the lake of the same name and offers a look at some diverse animal and plant species; the Le Fourchu trail (4.4 km loop), which leads to Lac Castor and to the Rivière Fourchue, includes some beautiful views. At press time the centre was closed. It is expected to reopen under new management soon, but be sure to call ahead first.

Access: Highway 20, Exit 488. Route 289, 16 km south of Saint-Alexandre.
☎ (418) 495-2153

■ CEF de Macpès

The Centre Éducatif Forestier (CEF, Forestry Education Centre) de Macpès, located south of Rimouski on the shore of Lac Malfait, has some beautiful small self-guided nature trails. Each month a different activity is highlighted. For example, during the month of September, workshops and arts and crafts activities are offered for children aged from four to seven years.

There are 5.4 km of trail: three self-guided nature trails. The Les Pessières trail (1.1 km loop) goes around Lac du Mélèze; the Les Cédrières trail (2.1 km loop) leads to a beaver pond; and the Étang trail leads to two beautiful lookout points on Lac Malfait. At press time the centre was closed. It is expected to reopen under new management soon, but be sure to call ahead first.

Access: from Rimouski take Route 232 to Sainte-Blandine; 4 km after this town, take the 3ᵉ Rang Ouest to the centre.
☎ (418) 735-2266

■ Other Hikes, Walks and Discoveries in the Bas-Saint-Laurent Region

• Halte Écologique des Battures de Kamouraska, an ecological information centre on the Kamouraska sandbanks in Saint-André; trails, lookout points, ornithology, ☎ (418) 493-2514

- Parc à Chevreuils Richard Lynch, a deer park in Saint-Pacôme; have deer eating right out of your hands, ☎ (418) 856-5833

- Réserve Nationale de Faune de la Baie de L'Isle-Verte; guided hikes; trails along the sandbanks of the river, ☎ (418) 898-2757

- Île Verte; whale-watching on the north shore; visit the lighthouse and an old schoolhouse, ☎ (418) 898-2757

- Île aux Basques, facing the town of Trois-Pistoles; guided excursions and walks. Société Provancher, ☎ (418) 851-1202

- Musée de la Mer (sea museum) and Lieu Historique National de Pointe-au-Père National Historic Site; visit an old lighthouse and an exhibition on the sinking of the Empress of Ireland (1914), that claimed 1,012 lives, ☎ (418) 724-6214.

Gaspésie

This region at the eastern extremity of Québec has gained almost mythical proportions. People dream of doing the tour of Gaspésie: discovering its magnificent coastal landscape, where the **Chic-Chocs Mountains** plunge abruptly into the cold waters of the St-Laurent; going all the way to the famous Rocher Percé; heading out to sea toward Île Bonaventure; visiting the extraordinary Parc Forillon and finally slowly returning through Baie des Chaleurs and the valley of the Rivière Matapédia in the hinterland. This beautiful corner of Québec, with its strikingly picturesque scenery, is inhabited by friendly fascinating people, who still rely mainly on the sea for their living. Most of Gaspésie's residents live in small villages along the coast, leaving the centre a vast region of dense Boreal forest. The highest peak in Southern Québec lies there, in the part of the Appalachians known as the Chic-Chocs Mountains.

■ Parc de la Gaspésie

Parc de la Gaspésie, created in 1937, used to be called "land of the twisted woods." With an area of 802 km², it has much to offer hikers. To begin with the atmosphere is fabulous, with the mountainous region divided between two large massifs, the Chic-Chocs and the McGerrigle mountains. The network of hiking trails, over 100 km in total, allows you to explore the high peaks of the park and enjoy views unlike any anywhere else in the world. Several of the trails can be completed with just a few hours of hiking.

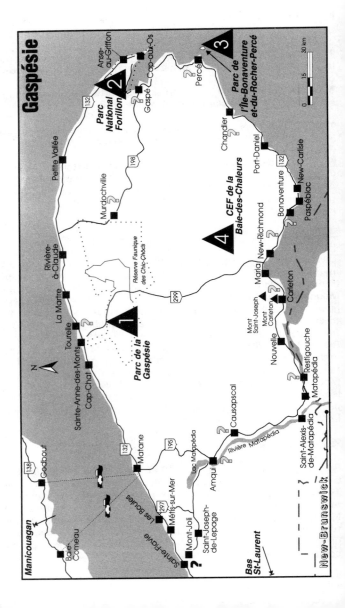

Large numbers of caribous, some 250 head, roam the park, more particularly **Mont Jacques-Cartier** (1,270 m). The Algonquin called the caribou *xalibu* which means "he who scratches the earth for food." This beast shares the territory with deer and moose, making Parc de la Gaspésie a unique phenomenon in North America. It is possible to cross four types of forest on one hike: a low altitude Boreal forest, an evergreen forest, a subalpine forest with dwarfed trees and, on the summits, the tundra with its moss and lichen.

The **Centre d'Interprétation de la Nature**, in the heart of the park, has a permanent exhibition. Some of the trails also start here. Guided hikes, discussion evenings, as well as several other activities are organized.

Along with the chalets, shelters and campsites available to hikers, there is the **Auberge le Gîte du Mont-Albert** for the more discerning hiker with a taste for fine cuisine.

Above all, remember to cover up and to wear proper footwear before hitting the trail of Parc de la Gaspésie. Snowstorms are common during spring and fall, and tracts of snow are often found here and there in the middle of summer!

Also note that the park offers a public transportation system to the starting points of several trails.

Access: Route 132 to Sainte-Anne-des-Monts, then Route 299 for 40 km to the Centre d'Interprétation (information centre).
☎ (418) 763-3301, 763-7811
Gîte du Mont-Albert ☎ 1-800-463-0860

Mont Jacques-Cartier

Level of Difficulty:	◿◿
Total Distance:	*8.2 km return*
Change in Altitude:	*477 m*
Starting Point:	*the La Galène shelter parking lot (Route 14), then by shuttle to the parking lot at the foot of Mont Jacques-Cartier. The bus service also picks up people at the Centre d'Interprétation (information centre) in season.*

Mont Jacques-Cartier is the highest summit in southern Québec at 1,270 m. The La Montée trail, which leads to the summit, is quite difficult but not very long — less than two hours of walking. There is a lean-to and an observation tower at the summit.

The view is mesmerizing from the summit of Mont Jacques-Cartier (1,270 m): valleys, rounded peaks, and the beautiful massif of the McGerrigle Mountains stand out. Your best chance to see caribous is at the summit of Mont Jacques-Cartier. Return by the same trail.

Mont Albert

Level of Difficulty:	◿◿◿
Total Distance:	*13 km return*
Change in Altitude:	*885 m*
Starting Point:	*Centre d'Interprétation (information centre).*

The trail climbs steeply up to the opening, called the *Éclaircie*, where the trees become smaller. The area from here to the summit of Mont Albert consists of tundra and a vast 20 km² plateau. The northern summit (1,083 m), which is reached after three hours of hiking, has a lean-to. Return by the same trail.

Variation: It is possible to continue on the trail and head back down on the La Vallée trail, forming an almost 17 km-loop.

Mont Richardson

Level of Difficulty:	◿◿
Total Distance:	*11.6 km return*
Change in Altitude:	*610 m*
Starting Point:	*Mont Richardson parking lot, on Route 160 (by Route 16).*

The trail to follow is called Les Cailloux. Rather steep and difficult, it climbs up to the intersection with the trail to the summit of Mont Joseph-Fortin. It continues uphill to the summit of Mont Richardson (1,220 m) for a magnificent 360° view. Mont Albert and the McGerrigle chain await your contemplation. Return by the same trails.

Variation: A tour of Mont Joseph-Fortin, which also offers a spectacular view, is possible on the way back down. This detour will add 3 km to the total distance.

Lac aux Américains

Level of Difficulty:
Total Distance: *2.6 km return*
Change in Altitude: *90 m*
Starting Point: *Lac aux Américains parking lot on Route 160 (by Route 16).*

The short and easy trail leads to Lac aux Américains, where an impressive cirque, a vestige of the ice age, spreads out at your feet. Return by the same trail.

Pic du Brûlé

Level of Difficulty:
Total Distance: *13.2 km loop*
Change in Altitude: *368 m*
Starting Point: *Parking lot at Lac-Cascapédia campsite on Route 11.*

The climb up is along the beautiful, wide-open Des Crêtes trail. There are several great views along the trail, up to the northern summit of Mont Ernest-Ménard (868 m), from where the view is mindblowing! The trail heads downhill for a bit, before climbing up to the summit of Pic Brûlé (792 m). From there, leave the Des Crêtes trail to return down toward Lac Cascapédia by the L'Orignal trail, formerly a forestry road.

Note: The Des Crêtes trail is a long-hike trail (40 km) from east to west across a portion of the Chic-Chocs.

McGerrigle Trail

Level of Difficulty:
Total Distance: *23 km (one way only)*
Change in Altitude: *1,070 m*
Starting Point: *the La Galène parking lot, then by shuttle to the foot of Mont Jacques-Cartier, or by bus from the Centre d'Interprétation (information centre) to the foot of Mont Jacques-Cartier.*

This trail usually takes two days of hiking with an overnight in the Tétras shelter (or three days with overnights in the Tétras and Roselin shelters.)

Day 1 (9 km): The first day's hike covers the 477 m up to the magnificent summit of Mont Jacques-Cartier (1,270 m) for a panoramic view. The trail then heads down to the southwest around Mont Comte before arriving at the Tétras shelter located near Lac Samuel-Côté.

Day 2 (14 km): From the shelter the trail climbs for a bit to the summit of Mont Xalibu (1,130 m), which means "caribou" in Algonquian. There is a fantastic view of Lac aux Américains, Mont Albert and the valley of the Rivière Sainte-Anne, from the summit. The trail heads right down to the shore of Lac aux Américains where you can admire a magnificent cirque, left over from the ice age. The trail finally heads straight downhill to the park's Centre d'Interprétation de la Nature, or information centre.

■ **Parc Forillon**

Parc National Forillon, located on the northeastern point of the Gaspé peninsula, takes up an entire peninsula jutting into the sea.

Cliffs sculpted by the sea, coves, beaches and capes create the kind of striking landscape you would imagine at the end of the world.

Along with the numerous aquatic birds, whales and seals also swim in the waters off these shores.

Visit the **Phare du Cap-des-Rosiers** (☎ 418-892-5613), an old lighthouse, built in 1858 and declared a historic monument. At 37 m, it is the highest lighthouse in Canada.

There are more than 50 km of trails in the park, 36 km of which are reserved for hiking.

Access:	Route 132 to Cap-aux-Os.
	☎ (418) 368-6050
	To reserve a campsite: ☎ (418) 368-5505

A Tour of the Area

Level of Difficulty:	⌂
Total Distance:	*3 km loop*
Change in Altitude:	*75 m*
Starting Point:	*Grande-Grave parking lot.*

This small self-guided trail, in the Grande-Grave sector, explains the history of the inhabitants of Forillon.

Les Graves

Level of Difficulty:	
Total Distance:	*13.2 km return*
Change in Altitude:	*90 m*
Starting Point:	*Anse-Blanchette (cove) parking lot.*

This trail follows the coast, through several coves, from Anse-Blanchette to Anse-Saint-Georges and then Anse-aux-Sauvages; it then climbs up a bit before reaching the end of the Forillon peninsula, at Cap-Gaspé, where a lookout point lets you take in the panoramic view. If you are lucky you may see some whales or seals. Return by the same trail.

Variation: For a shorter hike, you could park your car in Anse-aux-Sauvages. From there the return trip is 7.8 km.

Mont Saint-Alban

Level of Difficulty:	
Total Distance:	*8.5 km loop*
Change in Altitude:	*250 m*
Starting Point:	*parking lot at the Plage Petit-Gaspé (beach).*

This three-hour hike leads to the summit of Mont Saint-Alban (283 m). Several beautiful views and lookout points allow hikers to truly appreciate the fabulous landscape of Parc Forillon.

■ **Parc de l'Île-Bonaventure-et-du-Rocher-Percé**

Île Bonaventure resembles a whale from the coast. It was acquired by the government of Québec in 1971, and became a conservation park in 1985 to protect the colony (55,000) of gannets.

Île Bonaventure was inhabited for about a hundred years by Irish and Anglo-Normans.

Four trails, covering a total distance of 15 km, crisscross the island; and what better way to pass the day than in the company of the island's some 200,000 birds?

Access:	a ferry leaves for the island 3.5 km from the town of Percé.
	☎ (418) 782-2240

Tour of the Island

Level of Difficulty:
Total Distance: *8.4 km loop*
Change in Altitude: *120 m*
Starting Point: *from the pier.*

The ferry to Île Bonaventure drops passengers off at the cove Anse à Butler, where the Accueil (visitor information centre) is located. A short visit here includes an exhibition of the flora, fauna and history of the island as well as a visit to the historic house, the Maison Bouthillier.

The Tour of the island starts on the Mousses trail, which crosses the northern part of the island and enters the eastern side of the preservation zone, known as the "hidden face of the island." Thousands of birds rub shoulders here. From where the trail follows the cliffs to where it ends in pretty Baie des Marigots, it is known as the Chemin-du-Roy. The trail crosses a former residential area, where the old houses are reminiscent of the days gone by, before returning to Anse à Butler.

■ CEF de la Baie-des-Chaleurs

The Centre Éducatif Forestier (CEF, Forestry Education Centre) de la Baie-des-Chaleurs is located north of New Richmond, on the shore of the Rivière Petite-Cascapédia. A covered bridge, a lush atmosphere and varied plant life make up this centre in log-driver- (*draveur*) country.

There are 11.3 km of trails, with three self-guided trails and one hiking trail: the Calypso (1.8 km) and Ruisseau (2.3 km) trails follow the Rivière Petite-Cascapédia, while the Le Giboyeux hiking trail completes a 5-km loop. At press time the centre was closed. It is expected to reopen under new management soon, but be sure to call ahead first.

Access: Route 132 to Richmond. From there take the small road that leads to the town of Saint-Edgar, 11 km north of New Richmond.
☎ (418) 392-4468

■ Other Hikes, Walks and Discoveries in the Gaspésie Region

● Centre d'Interprétation du Saumon Atlantique (Atlantic salmon information centre), in Sainte-Flavie ☎ (418) 775-2969

● Jardins de Métis, in Grand-Métis; classified among the most beautiful gardens in the world, ☎ (418) 795-2221

- Réserve Faunique de Matane; trail leading to the summit of Mont-Blanc (1,065 m), ☎ (418) 562-3700

- Centre d'Interprétation du Vent et de la Mer, an information centre of the wind and the sea, in Cap-Chat, ☎ (418) 786-5507

- Centre d'Interprétation des Phares, a lighthouse information centre, in La Martre, ☎ (418) 288-5698

- Réserve Faunique de Port-Daniel; trail along the Rivière Port-Daniel, ☎ (418) 396-2789

- The Grotte de Saint-Elzéar and the Musée des Cavernes à Saint-Elzéar; guided visits of the oldest grotto in Québec, ☎(418) 534-4335

- Parc de Miguasha, near De Nouvelle; numerous fossils, ☎ (418) 794-2475

- The Chutes (waterfalls) and the Marais (swamp) in Causapscal; salmon observation, ☎ (418) 756-3670

The Îles-de-la-Madeleine

Lying in the centre of the gulf of the St-Laurent, the archipelago known as the Îles-de-la-Madeleine contains a dozen islands, spread over 65 km. Half of the islands are connected to each other by sand dunes, while more than 300 km of sandy beaches blend into an almost tropical landscape. And to top it off, warm waters are comfortable enough for swimming!

There are no big mountains, **Big Hill** (174 m) is the tallest summit of the islands. No marked network of trails has been developed, but there are hillocks, coves, dunes, lagoons, beaches, cliffs, caves, bays and points to explore to your heart's content. It is also virtually impossible to get lost on the islands: paths, hills and beaches always lead to a familiar place. Like *Madelinots* (as residents of the islands are called) say, "you can see the sea from every house." The residents are renowned for their hospitality and will often gladly take you back to your starting point if you get lost. Birdwatchers take note: close to 200 species of birds frequent the islands.

Association Touristique des Îles-de-la-Madeleine : ☎ (418) 986-2245

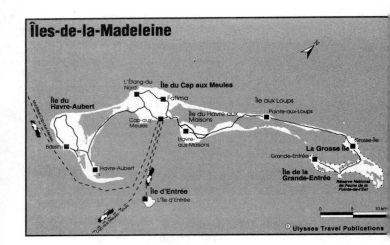

The following is a list of the main hiking spots:

■ Île du Havre Aubert

- The Anse-à-la-Cabane lighthouse, in Bassin
- The ridges and the mountain, along the numerous little paths; this is the biggest forest on the islands
- La Grave (pebble beach), in Havre-Aubert
- The western dune
- The dune in Havre aux Basques

■ Île d'Entrée

- Chemin Mountain and along the cliffs
- Summit of Big Hill (174 m)

■ Île du Cap aux Meules

- Chemin de la Mine (in Cap-aux-Meules)
- From the Étang-du-Nord (north pond) to Cap du Phare (lighthouse cape)

- Stroll along the superb cliffs of Belle-Anse at Cap au Trou (Fatima)
- Climb to the summit of Butte du Vent, a ridge
- Take a guided hike through a unusual landscape of dunes with group leaders from Attention Frag'Iles, ☎ (418) 986-6644

■ Île du Havre aux Maisons

- Tour around the ridge, Butte Mounette
- Climb the ridge, Butte Ronde
- Head out to the small lighthouse on Chemin des Échoueries
- Walk along Chemin des Montants
- Walk the length of the southern dune beach, Plage de la Dune du Sud and stroll along the edge of the red cliffs and the caves
- From Pointe-aux-Loups, cover the northern dune beaches, Plage de la Dune du Nord and Plage de la Pointe-aux-Loups

■ La Grosse Île

- Walk out to Rockhill Point
- Hike the trails of the Réserve Nationale de Faune de la Pointe-de-l'Est, a national wildlife reserve; stroll along the beach, Plage de la Grande Échouerie
- Walk around Old Harry Point (superb cliffs)

■ Île de la Grande Entrée

- Walk around Pointe de la Grande Entrée and its magnificent fishing port
- Stroll along the short trail on Île Boudreau
- Take a guided hike (nature interpretation) with group leaders from Club Vacances Les Îles, ☎ (418) 985-2833

Manicouagan

Covered by thick Boreal forest, Manicouagan also has an extensive river system that powers the eight generating stations of the Manic-Outardes hydro-electric complex.

Parc Régional de Pointe-aux-Outardes is a haven for nature and outdoor enthusiasts, who come to observe a multitude of bird species and to adventure in the Groulx Mountains.

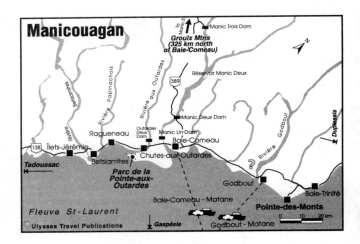

■ The Groulx Mountains

The Groulx Mountains are located 325 km north of the city of Baie-Comeau, on Route 389. The route to get there passes by the Daniel-Johnson (Manic-Cinq) Dam and the Manicouagan Reservoir. It is 1,100 km from Montréal to this mountain chain.

Some hiking, but mostly cross-country skiing treks, began to develop in the region as of 1986, after the extension of Route 389 to Labrador.

Several of the summits of the Groulx Mountains are over 1,000 m high, making this the third highest mountain chain in Québec, after the Torngats and the Laurentides. The highest summit of the chain is Mont Veryier, at 1,104 m.

Valleys, high plateaus and massifs make up the terrain of the Groulx Mountains. A few short and long hiking trails have been laid out. There is a parking lot and campsite along the side of Route 389 (at km 117). Farther into the forest, a shelter, two lean-tos and a tent platform have been set up for hikers.

A long hike of 44 km can be done completely independently. This expedition takes one week to complete and demands a certain knowledge and experience (maps and compass) from the hiker. It is also possible to establish a base camp and do day hikes up to the neighbouring peaks.

The tundra reigns supreme in these parts and most hikes are across moss-covered terrain. Several superb views of the region, particularly of the Manicouagan Reservoir, add to the hikes across the plateaus.

Those who wish to hire a guide should contact Thoseure Nomade, ☎ (819) 842-4302 or 821-5488.

■ Other Hikes, Walks and Discoveries in the Manicouagan Region

- Parc Régional de Pointe-aux-Outardes; significant birdwatching site (200 species); hiking trails, ☎ (418) 567-4227

- Phare de Pointe-des-Monts; museum, historic lighthouse (1830), houses a bed and breakfast and country kitchen restaurant, ☎ (418) 939-2332, 589-8408

Duplessis

People visit the Duplessis region to relish the peace and quiet as well as the rich flora and fauna. There are also of course the splendours of Île d'Anticosti and the stunning Archipel de Mingan.

■ Île Grande Basque

Île Grande Basque is part of the Parc Régional de l'Archipel des Sept Îles, located in the Fleuve St-Laurent just in front of the city of Sept-Îles. The park includes several islands including Île Corosol, one of the largest reserves for migratory birds in Canada.

Île Grande Basque is 4.5 km long and 2 km wide, and is accessible by ferry. Nine hiking trails crisscross the island for a complete tour. Hikers can stay overnight at one of the ten campsites.

Access: a ferry links the island to Parc du Vieux-Quai in Sept-Îles. ☎ (418) 968-1818 or 962-1238

Tour of Île Grande Basque

Level of Difficulty:
Total Distance: *9 km loop*
Change in Altitude: *100 m*
Starting Point: *Accueil (visitor centre), near the*
                                   arrival pier.

The tour of Île Grande Basque is relatively easy to complete since the change in altitude is minimal. The island is overflowing with peaceful spots, so plan to stop several times along the way. Coves, capes, points, reefs, stone ramparts, peat bogs, grottos, waterfalls and faults await discovery.

The trail loops around the entire island along ten small trails, named after animals. Several beautiful viewpoints along the way give out onto the bay, the neighbouring islands and the city of Sept-Îles. The hike up to the summit with the large lookout point (150 m) by the La Perdrix (partridge) trail, as well as the one up to the smaller lookout point (80 m) by the La Mouette (gull) trail, offer some beautiful panoramas.

■ Île d'Anticosti

Île d'Anticosti, located at the mouth of the Fleuve St-Laurent, south of Havre-Saint-Pierre, is 222 km long and 56 km wide.

This immense island, with an area of 7943 km², belonged for many years to a chocolate maker from France, named Henri Menier. He acquired the island in 1895, planning to make it his own personal hunting and fishing ground! He populated the island with animals, bit by bit: beavers, moose, caribous, hares, white-tailed deer. This last animal adapted so well to the island's territory, that it numbers around 125,000 today.

Île d'Anticosti has belonged to the Québec government since 1974, however recreational hiking has only been practised here since 1986. Huge beaches, cliffs, canyons, waterfalls, escarpments, shipwrecks and rivers make up the magnificent atmosphere.

Several hikes, from a couple of hours to several days, can be done.

Hikes and Sights on Île d'Anticosti

- The canyon of Chute Vauréal (76 m) waterfall
- Rivière de la Patate and its caves
- Rivière Sainte-Marie

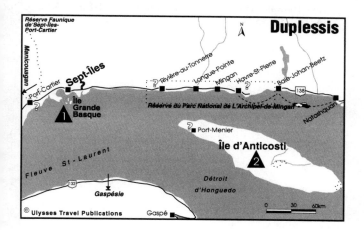

- Rivière la Loutre and the Faillette Brown wreck
- Pointe de l'Ouest and the Calou wreck
- The cliffs of Baie de la Tour
- Observation canyon, bay and cape
- Chute à Boulé waterfall
- Baie MacDonald
- Pointe Carleton and the Wilcox wreck

For information and reservations (accommodation, guided hikes, mountain bike rentals, etc.) : SEPAQ Anticosti, ☎ 1-800-463-0863 or (418) 535-0156.

Guided hikes: Randonnées Plein Air, ☎ (514) 528-1730; Safari Nature, ☎ (514) 441-9560.

■ Other Hikes, Walks and Discoveries of the Duplessis Region

- Réserve Faunique de Sept-Îles-Port-Cartier; several hiking trails; see Lac Walker and Chute MacDonald (waterfall), ☎ (418) 968-1401

- Parc de la Rivière-des-Rapides, near Sept-Îles; hiking trails

- Réserve du Parc National de l'Archipel-de-Mingan; spectacular rock formations (monoliths); a must-see, ☎ 1-800-463-6769 or (418) 538-3331

GLOSSARY

■ **Hiking Vocabulary**

Bergschrund :   a crevasse or gap at the head of a glacier, also called rimaye

Bivouac :   a temporary open camp without tents

Cairn :   a pile of rough stones arranged at the summit, or along a trail indicating the way

Chimney :   narrow vertical fissure in a rock-face, used by mountaineers to ascend

Cirque :   a deep bowl-shaped hollow with steep sides and a sloping floor formed by glaciers, also called a corrie

Col :   a depression in the ridge connecting two mountains, often providing a pass from one slope to another

Crest :   the top of a mountain

Crevasse :   a deep open crack, usually in a glacier

Dièdre :   a large shallow corner in a rock face

Gaiters :   the waterproof coverings extending from the ankle to the instep, usually strapped under the foot, worn to prevent snow, mud, pebbles from entering the boot

Gully :   a water-worn ravine, through which avalanches pass

Knob :   a small rounded hill or knoll

Ledge :   a narrow shelf-like rock projection from a mountain or side of a cliff

Massif :   a compact mass of rocks forming the peaks of a mountain range

Marker :   anything indicating the trail to follow such as paint markings on trees or rocks

Moraine :	a mass of rocks and debris carried by glaciers and forming ridges when deposited
Névé :	an expanse of porous, granular snow, not yet formed into ice at the head of a glacier, also called firn
Overhang :	the overhanging part of a rock formation on a cliff or mountainside
Pitch :	the steepness of a mountain slope over a distance
Ridge:	the intersection between two rock faces
Scree :	the small loose stones that accumulates at the foot of a cliff or slope
Sérac :	a steep pointed tower of ice among crevasses on a glacier
Through-route :	the horizontal progression through a rock face
Timberline :	a tree-growth limit above which trees are less than 2 m high

■ French Terms or Expressions Related to Hiking

Abri:	lean-to
Anse:	cove
Arête:	edge, ridge
Auto-Interpétation:	self-guided (trail)
Balise:	marker
Batture:	sandbank
Bosse:	knob
Boucle:	loop
Carte:	map
Centre d'Acceuil:	visitor centre

Centre d'Interprétation:	information centre
Cheminée:	chimney
Chute:	waterfall
Couloir:	gully
Crête:	comb, ridge
Étang:	pond
Falaise:	cliff
Faune:	fauna
Fleuve:	river
Flore:	flora
Garde:	ranger
Grimpant:	climbing
Ligne supérieure de la forêt:	timberline, treeline
Littoral:	coast
Longueur:	pitch
Marais:	swamp
Mare:	pond
Plage:	beach
Pic:	peak, summit
Randonneur:	hiker, backpacker
Randonnée pédestre:	hiking
Rang:	former siegneurial road, still used as roads today

Rebord:	ledge
Refuge:	(with services): lodge; (withoutservices): shelter
Réserve Faunique:	wildlife reserve
Rocher:	boulder
Route de bûcheron:	lumber road
Ruisseau:	stream
Saillie:	ledge
Sentier:	trail
Sommet:	summit, peak

Answers to Quiz on p 14

1-T	11-F	21-T
2-F	12-T	22-F
3-F	13-T	23-T
4-T	14-T	24-F
5-T	15-F	25-F
6-T	16-F	26-T
7-F	17-F	27-T
8-F	18-F	28-F
9-F	19-F	29-F
10-F	20-T	30-T

INDEX

■ ULYSSES TRAVEL GUIDES

☐ Affordable Bed & Breakfasts
in Québec . . . . $9.95 CAN
$7.95 US

☐ Canada's maritime
Provinces . . . . $24,65 CAN
$12,95 US

☐ Dominican Republic
2nd Edition . . . . $22.95 CAN
$14.95 US

☐ Guadeloupe . . . . . . $22.95 CAN
$14.95 US

☐ Martinique . . . . $22.95 CAN
$14.95 US

☐ Montréal . . . . $19.95 CAN
$12.95 US

☐ Ontario . . . . $14.95 CAN
$12.95 US

☐ Panamá . . . . $22.95 CAN
$14.95 US

☐ Provence -
Côte d'Azur . . . . . $24,95 CAN
$12,95 US

☐ Québec . . . . $24.95 CAN
$14.95 US

☐ El Salvador . . . . $22.95 CAN
$14.95 US

■ ULYSSES GREEN ESCAPES

☐ Hiking in the Northeastern
United States . . . . $19.95 CAN
$12.95 US

☐ Hiking in Québec . . $19.95 CAN
$12.95 US

■ ULYSSES DUE SOUTH

☐ Cartagena (Colombia) . $9.95 CAN
$5.95 US

☐ Montelimar (Nicaragua) $9.95 CAN
$5.95 US

☐ Puerto Plata - Sosua - Cabarete
(Dominican Republic) . . $9.95 CAN
$5.95 US

■ ULYSSES TRAVEL JOURNAL

☐ Ulysses Travel Journal $9.95 CAN
$5.95 US

QUANTITY	TITLES	PRICE	TOTAL
		Sub-total	
		Postage & Handling	3.00 $
		Sub-total	
		G.S.T. in Canada 7 %	
		TOTAL	

Name : _____

Address : _____

City : _____

Postal Code : _____

Payment : ☐Money Order ☐Visa ☐MC ☐Cheque

Card Number : _____

Expiry Date : _____

Signature : _____

ULYSSES
TRAVEL PUBLICATIONS

4176, Saint-Denis
Montréal, Québec
H2W 2M5
Tel : (514) 843-9882
Fax: (514) 843-9448